JOY COMES IN THE MORNING

Writing Through Darkness at the Julian Center for Domestic Violence

Edited by Rachel Sahaidachny

Joy Comes in the Morning: Writing Through Darkness at the Julian Center for Domestic Violence

Editor: Rachel Sahaidachny
Book Design and Layout: Andrea Boucher

ISBN: 978-0-9967438-6-0

Printed in the United States of America

INwords PUBLICATIONS
PRESENTED BY THE **INDIANA WRITERS CENTER**

The Julian
Center

INDIANA WRITERS CENTER
BE A WRITER

ALLEN WHITEHILL CLOWES CHARITABLE FOUNDATION

**INDIANA ARTS
COMMISSION**
MAKING THE ARTS HAPPEN

WITH SUPPORT FROM:
ARTSCOUNCIL
AND THE CITY OF INDIANAPOLIS

ART WORKS.

**National
Endowment
for the Arts**
arts.gov

BUTLER | JORDAN COLLEGE
of the ARTS

• Art by Stevie Richardson •

Table of Contents

Introduction

The Julian Center provides shelter and support for victims of domestic violence and sexual abuse. A safe space is step one of the many steps survivors must take to reclaim their self-sufficiency. Writing is one way to begin to understand their own stories, minds, and hearts. It is tough work, and often the workshop participants came to class for the week shocked and disappointed that they had not been able to make time and space for writing on their own.

We met every week for eight weeks. There was a daytime group and an evening group. Some individuals showed up regularly and never missed a session; others came only once, but went so deep into their own interior that they surprised themselves with what they had to say. Often after a writing session, the women would share what they had discovered or written. Giving voice to their own stories helped them reclaim a part of themselves that had been buried under all the stress and fear.

It was clear from the first workshop meeting that safety and security are of the utmost concern to the participants as they recover from past trauma and abuse. Sometimes when a survivor enters the shelter she must give up her real name and choose a new one for safety. Many of the writers chose not to use their names in the book. Some of the authors' names are represented with an initial for privacy, and though some of the initials are the same, each is a different individual.

The phrase I chose for the title, "Joy comes in the morning," is from the story of Quindara Lovings. It so well represents the hope the workshop participants have—that they will get through this awful pain and anger. They will be strong and belong to themselves and stay away from the abusers. Many of the women wrote about birds as a powerful symbol for the future. They want to be free to fly, to escape the pain.

The art selected for the book was created by one of the workshop participants, Stevie Richardson. In her writing Stevie observes that art therapy helped her to see that "this isn't the end for me." I'm grateful to use her prints for the cover and interior.

Trauma is sneaky and ensnaring. Leaving it behind is tough work. Some writers chose to confront it, and some preferred to leave it in the past. Both Belle Noche and Ms. C. wrote about the dark side of looking back, as though the past were a shroud that could cover them up. Many of the women didn't know how to see into the past without hurting. They felt unloved, destructive, and flushed with regrets and pain; but they also felt strong, brave, and determined to heal.

Someone once described the effects of trauma on the brain in a way that made me realize it is not just an emotional condition, but an actual alteration of the self. If someone is burned badly in a fire, you see the scars on the body and know the person has suffered something extreme. The same thing happens when someone is abused or experiences or witnesses traumatic events: a scar forms in the brain. The more trauma occurs, the more the brain is altered, the more the personality of the person is changed, and the more their perception of reality is reformed. The brain creates its own shield of defenses. Wounds and memories live on in the body. For the sake of protection, the mind will try to forget, to black out and cause the memories' images to fragment.

In some of the stories, the syntax is broken or interrupted. I've left it this way because communication can be a real struggle for a victim of abuse as she works through her perceptions of self and reality and sifts through the impact of trauma on her mind.

But there isn't only pain in this book. There is also creativity, self-worth, discovery, and love. What each writer really wanted to understand was how to love and be loved without abuse and pain. And I could see that these women were on their way to healing and love, because they were learning how to love and forgive and reclaim themselves.

Rachel Sahaidachny
Editor, Indiana Writers Center

I release you, my beautiful and terrible fear.
I release you.
~Joy Harjo

we're wrong about scars
they're not where we got hurt, they're
the places we healed
~Mike Cecconi

I MIGHT BE SHAKESPEARE'S SISTER

Belle Noche

Family Heirloom

THE SECOND TIME MY HEART was broken was by my mom. I had already been back in her life for three months and I hated it. She was always really mean, hateful and spiteful towards me, but lately it had been at an all-time high. She would always tell me how ugly, stupid, and worthless I was, and it finally registered how much she hated me. I know that I wasn't a good daughter for her and that I am always a reminder of my *father's* hate, and her regrets. But how could you do that to your own child? I am half of her and a quarter of her legacy, and she hates me more than anything. What hurts the most is that I love her and I love myself. How could she hate herself by hating me? I loved her unconditionally from the moment she pushed me out. I love her more than I love myself and she hates me. And if she hates me I hate me. I hate myself more and more every day because she does, because I am part of her and in the end, she hates part of herself. I forgive my mother and myself, but I will not allow her not to love me anymore. She should love everything that comes from herself, whether she likes it or not. I will not allow her to not love herself anymore. I believe that this vicious dance can be tamed and formed into a beautiful waltz. I will accept nothing less.

Know It All

I AM THE...BIRD,
Any bird will do. Big,
small, in the air or in the
the sky, I love them all.
I love how the penguin
does its funny walk.
Or how the ostrich stands tall
and stares you right in the eyes.
The swan is lovely and
graceful, and canaries
are always willing to
put on a spectacular show.
The owl always asks the one word
everyone wants to know.
And the peacock has that
confidence that puts models to shame.
I'm named after a bird so I
guess they have my favor.

Wishful Thinking

SOMETIMES I WONDER HOW THINGS could be if everyone was more self-aware. You could still have the same personality, disposition, and attitude but would be more careful about the things that you say, how you say them, and why you say them. But then I always question if we could or would be individuals anymore.

Or maybe it could be the one thing that everyone has in common besides living, having goals, and dying. A lot of times, I am too self-aware. I think that's the one thing that people see in me that makes them mistreat me. My self-awareness makes me easy prey and by the time I figure it out, I have already been ensnared, devoured, and passed off, becoming the dirt, then the plant, and then the mouse that eats the plant, and so on in a never ending food chain. It's funny, because I am at the beginning weak and helpless, and at the end strong and more rounded. Maybe this time I will be at the top of the food chain, only this time I will be vegan.

Alarm Clock

I REMEMBER...THE FIRST TIME my heart was broken. I was twenty and still at home with my mom. In July of 2012, I went to visit my mom and brother for the summer and ended up staying for good. My grandmother, back in Michigan, told me not to come back if I went to visit my mother. She was still angry about me being in foster care and how my mom treated me and then abandoned me to move to Indiana. I didn't think much of it at the time, but looking back on it only a few days later made me sad, lonely, and helpless. And ever since then I have been angry, bitter, sad, and curious. Hell, ever since I was four I felt those emotions and they have never lessened. The feelings only grew stronger, and I have found myself heartbroken and forgotten again and again and again. Maybe I really am a caged bird, forever forgotten and left behind. The good thing about that is that I always get out. The bad and most depressing thing about that is I always find my way back in. This time in a newer, smaller cage. My wings are clipped and a cover is always over me and my cage. And I'm still smiling, breathing, and living on the outside but crying, suffocating, and dying on the inside. It's kind of like Monopoly but I'm the game being played. Hopeless hope and chance with traps.

Whispers

I REMEMBER...THE FIRST TIME I started reading. I was four or five and it was just me and my mom at the time. We lived in Minneapolis and everything was good, life was great. I could read simple picture books, magazines, or different books with poetry. My parents didn't know that I could think, and I learned that I could understand complex concepts more easily than they. This was before Mom went crazy. I really used to look up to her and try to impress her with how smart I was and how proud I could make her. My dad was never around and we lived in a nice two-bedroom apartment, a few doors from my grannie and great grandmother and down the street from my favorite aunt. I would always read out the names for streets, buildings, cars, you name it, I could read it. Even though I never got the praise I was looking for, it paid off. In grade school and middle school I excelled, far above my peer reading level and all other levels too.

Dream Catcher

Sometimes I dream I'm on
Cloud Nine.
Looking at all the other
stars that make neat lines.
Watching all the
pretty birds fly by.
Relaxing and gazing in
the night time sky.
Sometimes I feel like Beyonce
'cause I'm wishing on a star.
Praying and wishing that all
of my dreams and goals take me far.
Taking me to a place where
all my nightmares disappear.

Seeing all of the peace and
serenity that can be found here.
Leading me back to a place
that's all right and just fine,
Taking me back to my new
Home on Cloud Nine.

Serendipity

THE SUN WAS SO BRIGHT, so vivid, it warmed the pain away. Yet their eyes glowed like fiends of the night. Life bloomed around us, but their eyes stuck out from the rotting cold faces. We made our bed amongst the flowers and the tall grasses. The clouds were our paramour, the moon and the stars were, too. Cold, gray, decomposing bodies surrounded us, mouths open and hungry, their stares piercing the afternoon sky. We shared one last kiss as they descended upon us. Fear was on our faces and it lingered on our skin, like the aroma of an impressive bouquet. These undead souls had made a lovely feast out of our physical beings as well as our thoughts and souls. As the moon came out and the stars twinkled in the night sky, we became one with the Earth, and the Earth welcomed us back into her sometimes cold embrace. But the cool, lifeless, indifferent bodies moved on, and continued the cycle anew.

Dollhouse

WELCOME TO OUR HUMBLE HOME. I hope you'll enjoy your stay, but first hear the rules you always must obey. Never draw back the curtains, don't let them see inside. Never let them see you cry or smile, emotions are weakness. Never gaze upon them with kind eyes, they'll tear you apart. But most of all, never trust anyone in this house, because we will all sell you out.

Lost and Found

Here lies all my wildest hopes and dreams.
Covered not with dirt but with hardened tears.
Buried deep within my shattered heart.
Replaced by others' greed and misery.
Gone like ships and planes in the Bermuda Triangle.
Waiting to be picked up from my mind's Lost and Found.
Slightly tattered but still good to use.
They just need some of life's laundry detergent;
and since I'm on a budget, the bargain kind.

Fire Starter

I am not just a woman.
I am an innovator, a goddess, a beacon of peace.
If man is a pillar of strength, I am the foundation of prosperity.
I am the brightest ray of sunshine, the loveliest blossom, the calm
before the storm.
I am not just fine, I am summertime fine.
I am powerful, and it shows.
I make the rules and everyone else just falls in line.
I am the stuff dreams are made of; you cannot touch me,
that's what you are afraid of.

Handle with Care

I WALK THE PATH TO my lost love. Traveling the long hard road
into darkness. Our love was brief; the time flew by so fast. Your
loving embrace still lingers on my skin. I can still hear your voice.
Deep down into the abyss I travel. My praises of your simple beau-
ty cower even the dastardly foe and bring tears to the coldest and
most unfeeling of souls. At last I have found you—my beloved,

my life. Shrouded in darkness, a shadow of your former self. The one that used to hold me and drown in my lyre's sweet grasp. Just a little while longer and we will be together at last. I need to be patient and wait before I turn to gaze upon you again. But my heart is weary and my eyes yearn for your image. And I turn around only to see you run back into the deep dark night. Never again will I see your smile, brighter than Apollo's chariot racing across the sky. Never will there be a voice so gentle, more beautiful than the notes sung by my lyre. Now all I feel are the beguiling eyes as they look over me in shame; the laments of all the animals, trees, and rocks that feel my pain. I was a fool to ever turn back before we walked onto Gaia's fertile soil, and now all of creation can see my choice. Goodbye Euridyce, my love, I have failed you twice. Goodbye for good my love, and good night.

Pick Me Up

LOOK INTO THE MIRROR AND gaze into the windows of your soul. See what has come to pass, the current trial and the long trip ahead. Wipe away the smudges of sorrow and let the light of life shine through. Fasten back the curtains that are holding you back, open the shutters that close off your emotions. Prop open the windows and let out the stagnant water, let the showers of healing pour in. Clean out your house and then you truly will be free. Windex only works for tangible things.

Time Travel

EVER SINCE I WAS A little girl, the concepts of time, life, and death were easy for me to understand. I remember watching flowers grow, bloom, and wilt for the first time. The thought that even humans could be born, live full or half lives, wilt like hot lettuce and then expire, was fascinating to me. We, as objects on this

Earth, whether it is a boy or a rock, are all made of matter and energy, neither of which can be destroyed or created, but recycled in a vicious and ironic dance. We all have our lines in this ever-changing script. Some of them start as moving soliloquies, while others end as tragic cameos. You could be the daughter of a world-traveling, hypocritical, pseudo-Kennedy, or an out-of-season orange as the result of choosing greenhouses over Mother Nature. What is important is how well you play your part in Life's play. And if you stand out enough for the world to remember you after you're gone.

All That Glitters
—A letter to my future self

IT'S BEEN SO LONG SINCE we have seen each other. I remember your tears after all the pain. Your gaunt face, eyes widened in shock, still haunts me. All of the bruises, the scars, the cuts, that burden we shared together. I remember how you always looked to the floor and never gazed at the sky, because the choice was made for you. And the times when I held you and dispelled your fears, knowing they would be a recurring issue. All the times you reeked of chamomile tea, hoping that sleep would take all of your problems away. The sound of your pained song was music to their ears. They took pride in catching you, little bird. Why did you let them? They took away your freedom, clipped your wings and made you their prisoner. My little bird all locked up in your gilded cage. Longing to be flying free, feathers caressed by the wind. Grow strong, little bird, and hang on just a little while longer. Plot your escape and keep your cover. Let your song be so beautiful that it makes them unlock the cage. Fly free, little bird, and don't look back. Leave behind your cage. It was a trap for the helpless.

Hey, little bird, the world is yours, fly on and take it.

Smoke, Fog, and Haze

IN THE BEGINNING, THERE WAS just fog. Deep and fragrant, it stretched out as far as the eye could see, farther than the mind reaches. Only those with a third eye have seen. While resting, I saw wisdom, peace, and supreme conquest. And when I opened my eyes, it all vanished. The fog turned to shade and everything turned black. But in the darkness there were faces: they had no mouths, no ears, no nose, only eyes. But their voices rang sharply through the air.

"Look forward," they said, and I did.

"Open your heart," they said. And I did. And, as I started to follow their directions, the darkness became light and things grew all around me.

"Move," they said, and I began to walk.

"Cry," they said, and tears began to run down my face, down onto the ground, and from them sprouted all of my memories; some good, some bad, reminders of my presence.

"Live," they said, and I began to falter because I never knew how to.

My life always belonged to someone else, and they lived for me. And then a hand reached out from behind me and pushed me forward, and the voices in unison said, "Breathe." And I inhaled deep and exhaled hard. And after that, I started to walk again and I never turned back. If I did turn back, a pillar of stone I would have become, like all of the voices of my past self behind me.

"Finally," they said, and I watched their spirits be released to manifest elsewhere as I moved on. This is how I began to heal. Not just physically or emotionally, but every facet of my being.

Closed Doors

THERE ARE TWO THINGS THAT I am certain of. One, time is fleeting and forgiving. Two, just because something has passed on doesn't mean it's completely gone. I know this to be true as I watched the sins from my former selves vanish from their spots on my soul. They were gone, but left stains that were easier to deal with than see. In order for me to live I had to stop surviving. To survive is only temporary and the means to do so can leave at any moment. But living is not enough, I must thrive. Letting go is never easy, so I have to leave it all behind. Abandon the hate, the rage, the shame. Close the door on guilt, and banish the pain. These things take time, and I have plenty. I am beginning to thrive and pave the way for a prosperous future. My past can no longer hurt me and my soul is clean. My mind is free and my heart is growing. Now the statues of my past emotions have their own exhibit. They are next to the paintings that are my memories, in the museum of my life. All of us can have our own museums of the past to reflect on if we just work hard and believe in ourselves.

IN A DARK PLACE

Ms. C

SOMEWHERE IN ME IS A dark place. You can't see it or touch it because it is so deep inside of my soul. I try to come out but I can't see my way, all the doors are locked up and I can't find the keys. Day after day, I search for the keys but they are nowhere to be found. I know if I find the keys I can let the light come in my soul and be happy again. In a dark place like this I can't let anyone in because they will lose the light inside their soul, like me, so I keep it locked and hide the keys from myself so no one can come in to see the real me in the real light. In a dark place I can hide from the world and be safe.

Don't Look Back

Don't look back there's
nothing there.

Don't look back: you won't
like what you might see.

Don't look back: you won't
like what you might hear.

Don't look back: you won't
like who you may meet.

Don't look back: you may not
like the plan you find there.

Just look forward
and find your future there.

Jesus Said

Jesus said: Come with me
and I will show you
all the things that I am.
Jesus said: follow me and
I will take you to a place
inside of my light.
Jesus said: love me and
I can teach you how to
love others and yourself.
Jesus said: trust me
and I will show you all
my many kingdoms of the
universe. Jesus said: come
live inside me and you will
never be alone again. Jesus said
come die with me and
you will never die again.

I JUST WANT PEACE

Chaunda Sumara Fabio

Wives submit yourselves unto your own husbands, as unto the Lord. Ephesians 5:22

IT WAS THIS SCRIPTURE HE would always use to defend his actions. I, myself, having been in ministry for years, have heard this scripture hundreds of times. I've heard it so much I now resent it.

"It's the word of God," how could I have issue with it? ...Yet, male-dominated religious institutions use it to keep women in abusive relationships.

I Remember

I REMEMBER SITTING IN THE car looking at him as he poured his heart out to me, thinking, "He can't be serious?" How is it after only one night out? It wasn't what I considered a date. Yet there he was pouring out his heart about how I made him feel and what type of man he was. Rather what he was pretending to be, an Ephesians Five man.

A majority of Christian women have asked the Lord for one in prayer. Did my ears perk up? You bet they did. He continued on and on and on and I just stayed silent. Finally, he shut up. Great, because I'm starting to think he's crazy. Then he turned to me and said, "So what do you think about all I've said?"

I wanted to say, "I think you're crazy," but I didn't. Instead, I quoted the New Testament by saying "I'm watching and praying." I could tell he didn't like my response. Really, what did he think? Was I to pour out love for someone I really didn't know?

I remember him kind of snorting, then turning away from me and looking out the window. He turned back and faced me, and then said, "Is that really what's on your mind?"

"Yes." I realized I needed to watch him. Who pours out their hearts out after one date? The crazy thing was, I didn't consider it a date even. We went out. We only went to Denny's—shit, what would he have said if I kissed him like he wanted?

I remember looking at him and how dark he appeared. It wasn't his actual complexion; it was his spirit. His eyes were yellow and discolored. They reminded me of the junkies back home.

"Jesus, who is this man sitting across from me?" I prayed.

He's a pastor. He couldn't possibly be on drugs. He's a man of God, or so he professes. He went back to talking about the type of husband he would be with the right "First Lady." I remember feeling insulted. I knew he was trying to bait me. "Not this sister!" I had to let him know that I'm not to be called First Lady.

Again, my reaction wasn't what he liked. But throughout my years in ministry, I've watched pastors, bishops, apostles, and men of the cloth bait and hook women with their ministry titles. Now I was on a wire internally, yet outwardly I remained calm.

Could it be that I was so hot, so holy, so intriguing that I just caused his heart to become inflamed?

If only...

Bee

Bumblebee, Bumblebee.
Oh, how I wish I could be thee
to fly despite my ability
yet I sit amongst my futility.

I don't know
just how those
claim to do
flying above natural barrier
flying no matter what
fly on bumblebee.
Maybe one day I can become thee.

Triumph

I remember making you Triumph.
You were the one I never thought
I could manage.
You offered yourself to me, knowing
I was afraid to handle thee.
Can you hold me?
Can you protect me?
Please don't let me die as I leave
To synchronize my life with thee.
My triumph.
He keeps me.

Better Not Bitter

It's what I'm determined to be.

I'm hurt.
I'm pissed.
I'll be damned if I'm going to let
you get the best of me.

Hurt
Pain
Depression
Despondency
I refuse to give in to your tendencies

~

I grieve what I could've been
The plans I made that would happen when…
When we would have our first child.
Oh, how I longed for motherhood.
Here I stand at the gravesite
I see the names of Will, Love, and Faith.
The seeds that never took root because of the trauma.
I remember all the blood
Praying it would stop.

What Happened?

HE HAS NERVE CALLING ME. He really said, "You continue to walk in an evil way." It's evil because I do not want to be married to an abusive man. I wonder how would his followers feel knowing all of his ways. He lies, cheats, and steals. He gambles and cannot keep his word. He NEVER studies the Bible unless he has a preaching engagement. He only knows seven scriptures and regurgitates them over and over.

I Remember NOT

IT WAS MORE LIKE GETTING hit with a baseball. I glanced at my mom all the while wondering why he had to bring this up, especially in front of her.

"Is it true?" *Don't ask me that.* "Is it?" *Agree with that question.*

"I don't remember," I responded. Here I was, little Miss Monkeyface again. Not the adult woman, the little girl being referred to as a monkey by those that claim they love her.

I remember the look on her face. Then she opened her mouth. *Please don't say something crazy.*

"Well, since you don't remember, it didn't happen." She turned to him, then asked him if he was taking his medicine.

I don't remember anything after that.

I don't remember the abuse, per se, yet there he was, sitting at the table asking my forgiveness. I DON'T REMEMBER.

"What's wrong with me? Who doesn't remember being sexually abused? No way, this really happened?" All these questions flooded my mind as he continued talking.

I remember my mom screaming. Oh, poor little Ms. Perfect Mother missed something. There goes her award out the window. That witch never paid attention to anything other than what was in her line of sight. I felt my hatred for her begin to rise. She was always about appearances. She talked about The Joneses, yet was so envious of them.

"Princess Jones got all A's in her classes."

"Princess Jones is so smart. You just need to try hard," on and on she would go.

The crazy thing is, though, I don't remember the actual incidents. I can recall when they began. I remember loving him, enjoying playing with him, then BOOM!

"I hate you! Get away from me!" I would yell.

I remember how my body would react whenever I was alone with him. Ugh! It was worse than "my skin was crawling." Even now I struggle to adequately describe it.

Crazy how Father reveals everything. Here I go to the bank to open a second checking account and find out he was writing bad checks on our joint account. He gave me some song and dance about why he had to close the account last year. I remember not believing him. Shit! I even remember sitting in Chase's parking lot trying to decide if I was going inside to speak to a banker. I didn't.

Why was I so determined to be in Egypt? Do you know that place? It is the place where DENILE (The Nile River) runs. Not waiting for the truth. Reality stinks just like in the movie *Matrix*. Why take the red pill?

"Come Celebrate with Me"

THIS WAS THE TITLE OF the invitation. I couldn't believe how many people had questions.

What the hell is wrong with people, I thought. If a friend invited me to a celebration, I would just show up. I swear I can't stand Hoosiers at times. I missed my girls: Shelly, Netta, Charlene, Kim, True Ride or Die, My BK Ladies. East Coast friends are way more loyal.

Not another damn text. I guess I shocked them when I told them "I revoke this invitation." You don't need to be in my new space.

I finally did it. I left him. No, like really left him.

Like a good Christian wife—I went back because of the medical issues with his back.

It was the darkest of nights. I hid out from those church folks. Don't ask me about Pastor. He has his Candy. That bitch should have took his old broke-down ass to the doctor. But no, I took an entire week off without pay.

Master Manipulation

I GLANCE AT MY PHONE to see the missed call from Pastor New-
bie. She has been the one he calls. I just wish she knew I don't
want to talk about him. I throw the phone in my purse and put
my car in gear.

I told her last time I don't want to hear about any conversation
they are having. She gave that excuse about not wanting me to
think anything that "isn't right." She was too late. The mere fact
that she has given him a listening ear has already caused her to kill
any positive thoughts I may have had about her. She claimed we
were friends. Friends don't hold twenty to thirty minute conversations with someone who wants to kill the other friend's character.
During the entire ride I just couldn't understand why she was calling me about him.

She left me a voicemail. I didn't listen to it at the time, but
I knew it was about him. It's not her wanting to gossip. She just
wants to be in "the know," I thought to myself. She would never
be a gossip.

Friends—who are they? Where is their loyalty?

I continue throughout my day, determined not to give him
nor her any mental space. A few days later I realize that I should
call her back. Why I felt a sense of obligation to her, I don't know.

Once again I'm in the car. Calling while driving limits the
amount of mess I'll have to endure, because I must reach my des-
tination. She answers and we exchange pleasantries. She couldn't
wait to bring him up. I tried to stop her; however, she shocked me.

She wanted to apologize to me. She began by retelling me
some of their last conversation, "He has all these things he's doing."

I remember zoning out, because I knew he was only trying to
hide his insecurities by building himself up to her.

"It's not true," was what brought me back to the present conversation.

I told her, "If his mouth was moving, he was lying." It's what he does. He wouldn't be a master manipulator if he didn't lie. She went on to state how it all came out through Facebook.

All I could think is, it's obvious he's your friend because they're on Facebook together. You can't be his friend and claim to be my friend as well.

She said, "My gosh, only the Lord knows what you've had to deal with being married to him."

I guess the light is finally starting to shine. He's been able to fool people for over half a decade. The sad truth is, he believes the lies and fake circumstances and situations he has in his head.

Q called me to let me know that she's my friend first. Yet, I met him through her and I know they still communicate. It's funny to me, because she's the reason he was introduced into my life. I also know that he's so handy that she wouldn't cut him off.

Yet what about loyalty?

I remember our introduction. Triumph, my car, had given up the ghost. He had the nerve to do it at Walmart. I drove him to get an oil change. When I returned they claimed they couldn't get him out of park. Now how in the world did that happen?

I jumped in the seat and couldn't get the clutch in reverse, but the car turned over. I can't tell you how many times I tried it, nor how many prayers I prayed while doing it.

Now what? Indy isn't like home. I couldn't just jump on a bus or train or even hail a cab to get home. Plus, I had my queen (Mom) with me. The auto department manager felt sorry for us, so he drove us home. I still thank the Lord for the favor. Customer service going above and beyond. Too bad he doesn't work there anymore.

I left my totally paid off car in the Walmart parking lot. Man, how I wished I never moved here. If I were home I could just pick up the phone and call my Uncle Jimmy. He was one of my dad's closest friends. I had secretly wished my mom and Uncle Jimmy would get together. My dad had passed in 1998. Aunt Lorie passed in 2000. They needed each other.

However, here I was with my queen and no Uncle Jimmy. I didn't worry because I was on spring break.

I just needed to clear my mind and think. I had no money, so I couldn't even get it towed. Plus, where was I going to have it towed to anyway? I had two weeks before I was set to report to my new school.

Day two and Triumph was still at Walmart. I had to do something. Q called saying, "Reverend Parker can fix your car." I took his information; however, I still had no money. I gathered from Google that, more than likely, I just needed a new clutch kit. Pretty simple fix, or so I thought.

I should have left his old broke-down ass in Georgia.

How did I allow myself to get swayed? I make a decision, I stick to that decision. Well, normally I would have.

Now I'm paying for it, literally.

Religious peer pressure, right is right, wrong is wrong.

The Bible is true, yet I struggle with real life application.

We met. He was a Reverend. A Pastor. He could be trusted…furthest thing from truth. He's a liar! He's a hypo-crit. He constantly wears a mask.

I had to travel for my business. He managed to worm his way in on my trip. I guess he didn't trust me.

I really did not want to babysit him. I was travelling for work, not pleasure. It was hard for him to save money, and plan a romantic getaway. He was too busy eating his seed everyday.

I talked it over with the other trainer, and she was OK with him coming along. I was nervous about introducing him to everyone. Sometimes he just interjects himself and his crazy opinions where it's not wanted.

When we get in the car I realize he won't let me drive. How controlling is that? I should have caught on with that clue.

The crazy thing is, it took longer to get there. He thinks he's such a good driver just because he drives for a living. He really wouldn't let me drive. He had the nerve to make comments about my driving.

Nothing I do is ever right. I'm starting to see the pattern.

We finally make it. I'm exhausted from all the talking he did in the car. We go to the local Kroger. He wants to cook. He really wants to show off. To the natural eye he's being kind.

I Just Want Peace

Longing for peace
You appear as a mirage
The more I run to you, the
Further you move away

Peace, oh how I desire your presence.

There was a time we walked in unity.
I remember when you would hold me close.
You even protected once.

~

Right is Right
Wrong is Wrong
If only life was black and white.

Reality is more a sea of gray.
The sea I swim in made of both tints, and tones, and shades of gray.

My arms are heaviest when I'm in the sea of shadow. The dark gray sea drags me out deeper and deeper.

PRAISING GOD FOR WHAT WE DID HAVE

Ms. Connie

M Y NAME IS CONNIE. I have always lived in Indianapolis, and never really thought much of leaving. I was brought up in a small community, Fountain Square, in a one-parent home with six siblings. We never had much, but we had what a lot of other families didn't have, and that was love. My mom did her best. We wore a lot of hand-me-down clothes, tailored by my mom.

I remember watching my mother from the kitchen door, always singing and praising God for what we did have, and that was each other. She would take the little we did have and make it into something amazing. She always was and will be my hero. If she got wind of the neighbors going hungry or our friends had very little themselves to eat, she would find a can of veg or sauce and add it to the meal and invite them over. Sometimes we ate with them at their place.

I started drinking at the age of thirteen when a painful part of my life came out in the open. The molestation stopped. My brother had molested me and my sisters for years.

I remember everything that happened that day: my brother was forcing himself on me, and my sister jumped on him. He beat her down, and I screamed out over and over. I thought he killed her. My mom just got home from work and heard me screaming. She saved us. My sister told her everything. But, because of what happened, I became a runner. I ran for years, in and out of life, and started drinking, just living place to place. The more I drank the more I ran. I hated myself. I hated the world I lived in. I lived in a make-believe world. I made the world I lived in.

I remember I lived out on the tracks. I lived in an abandoned field, because I knew if my brother ever tried it again, I could run.

After a few years of running I went back home to my momma and siblings, without my brother. I found my way back to school, and back to watching my momma from the kitchen door. When my momma invited me into the kitchen, that's when I found my passion. I wanted to be just like her—not just in the kitchen, but having children and raising them.

I never blamed my mom for the molestation. I blame my dad because if he didn't leave my momma and us kids behind to fend for ourselves, it might not have happened. I found out it happened to my brother, as well, from my dad's brothers.

MY STORY

Erin Allen

I Remember…

I remember the birth of my children.
I remember family vacations.
I remember being abused.
I remember being raped.
I remember being on drugs.
I remember being homeless.
I remember being scared.
I remember being afraid.
I remember family dinners.
I remember family outings.
I remember my dad.
I remember my great grandma.
I remember my grandma.
I remember being teased in school.
I remember being hungry.
I remember being in high school.
I remember when I was sad.

I remember trying to take my own life.

I remember feeling lost.

I remember feeling unloved.

I remember feeling like a burden.

I remember crying myself to sleep.

I remember being hurt.

I remember seeing my mom abused.

I remember living on the streets.

I remember not being able to take a shower.

I Remember Being Abused

I HAVE BEEN ABUSED SINCE the age of three. It started with me being sexually molested by my father. I was molested for four years. I was scared of my dad for a long time after that. I was emotionally abused all through school for being fat, short, ugly. I hated high school and dropped out in the tenth grade. I got into my first DV situation at age seventeen with a man that was twice my age. He was abusive in every way. He ended up being the father of my two kids.

I have had my head stuck in snow banks until I couldn't breathe, been beat around the house for hours. Hospitalized. Forced to have sex. Had all my money taken. I dealt with this for seven years, then went straight into another abusive relationship where I was forced to use drugs, beaten repeatedly, called names, controlled, raped in my sleep, dragged down the driveway with a car and left for dead. I was forced by gunpoint to transport drugs.

I have had numerous black eyes, bruises, broken bones, teeth knocked out, hair pulled and cut. I wanted to die instead of endure more abuse.

Leaving

LEAVING MICHIGAN IN AUGUST 2014 changed my life for the better. I was finally free from my abuser, or so I thought. He followed me, though, and after a week of being assaulted and raped over and over, I was able to find safety at a DV shelter. I had him arrested and sent to prison. That was the day my life changed.

Since being free from him I have gotten my health in order, taking care of things he wouldn't allow me to. I have lost weight and am getting my self-esteem back. I have stable housing, my independence, and my peace of mind back. All of this came from leaving Michigan and sending him to prison, going to WINGS, then Julian Center, and then Coburn Place. Thank you Indianapolis for giving me the chance to live for the first time.

Scars

MY SCARS ARE NOT JUST places I've been hurt and healed from. They are things I live with every day. Every day I have an ache or pain that was caused by one of the internal wounds I suffered at the hands of a man who claimed he loved me. I have some deep wounds and some physical elements I will NEVER heal from. I have chronic back pain from herniated discs in my back that are going to require surgery due to the injuries I have suffered.

Some scars heal in the physical sense, but take longer to heal in the mental form. Some internal wounds I can't say I will ever heal from, because I am reminded of them daily. Sometimes an event or something someone says can trigger a scar I thought was healed.

Being a survivor of domestic violence, sexual assault, date rape, and childhood molestation, and a recovering drug addict, I have days that scars I thought were healed are fresh wounds and feel like salt was thrown in them. I try to work through them and not let them bring me down, but some days that's harder than others.

Especially, when I have to see so many doctors for the injuries I've sustained, and knowing I will live the rest of my life in pain.

I'm working on healing my wounds through therapy, but dealing with PTSD, I don't know if my scars will ever be healed. I will continue to work on healing them. Sometimes I feel like I went through all this and continue to go through things to help others. I know I have a purpose for being here, I'm just not sure what that purpose is right now. But I will continue to push forward and keep pushing to heal the scars and wounds I have.

Being Kind

I AM TOO KIND, AND tend to get taken advantage of. People often take my kindness as a weakness. I am working on trying to be stronger and not give in so much, but it's hard. I often get used, abused, and taken advantage of, even in my friendships. I have a hard time telling people no, and that causes a lot of heartache and frustration on my end. People tend to take advantage of the kind-hearted. I have learned to set boundaries, but still have a hard time with them, and with saying no. So for me kindness causes a lot of heartache and sorrow, but I don't want to be unkind, either. I just wish I could find a happy medium. I am kind to others, but spend most days alone, crying, lonely, feeling unloved. There are so many times I want to just give up or go back to Michigan. I struggle every day, but nobody sees it because I am always smiling and doing for others, while on the inside I am crying and feel like I'm dying. I am extremely tired of feeling this way. I want peace and happiness in my life.

I Don't Remember

I don't remember not being abused.
I don't remember ever being happy.
I don't remember ever feeling true love.

I don't remember not being taken advantage of.
I don't remember not being in pain.
I don't remember life without medication.
I don't remember ever having a healthy relationship.
I don't remember ever being without doubt.
I don't remember ever being without guilt.

I Am a Dolphin

They are graceful and full of life.
They love to entertain.
I am very protective and nurturing like a dolphin.
I would love to be graceful in the water like they are.
I can be stubborn and bull-headed like they can be
When I don't want to do something.
But like the dolphin
I am a survivor
Even when all the cards are stacked against me.
I still come out on top.
I enjoy watching them both in captivity and the wild.
I would love to swim with them one day
They are so special to me.
I have a dolphin tattoo.
I love dolphins!

YOU CANNOT LIVE IN MY HEAD

Ms. J

I Remember...

I REMEMBER LIVING IN CALIFORNIA as a child. It was exciting to see the beach for the first time, and being in warm weather year-round. Exciting going to school at Sutter Jr. High, where I met my first Jewish friend.

I remember living in New York during the 1990s and how lovely the night life was. Seeing my friends who I went to school with grown up into adults. Getting my first apartment, how the hardwood floors looked. Being able to have my own bed that I bought. The first set of brand new dishes I wanted. Having cable turned on so I could watch whatever I wanted to.

I ordered pizza from La Nova's Pizza, had my best friend over to help me unpack. We stayed up as late as we wanted. Then the next day, going to the animal shelter and adopting a cat.

I remember moving from New York.

I remember the weather was cold, it had just snowed fifty-two inches. We stayed inside and made pizza, and watched *Halloween*. I don't remember the color of the carpets or what my neighbor looked like, or very much after that. Or what the landlord's name was.

I remember when I got saved. I knelt down on my knees and cried out to God to save me from the nightmare of the life I was living in. I repented my sins. I knew the life I had been living was a sin. My ex was not what God had planned for my life. I prayed and asked God to deliver me, and after renouncing and confessing my life changed. I began to know Jesus Christ as my Lord and Savior. It's been tough on me, because of the awakening that happened for me. To view everything for what it was—the Truth Movement. I found a pastor who talked with me and helped me get out of that mess. I just want the Lord Jesus Christ in my life.

I remember being a little girl playing with my sisters, dancing in the bedroom to Boy George. Then our step-father would come in and cuss...

My journey begins today with my feet firmly on the ground. Learning from all of yesterday, from hearing "I'm going to kill you," to hearing, "You can do this, it's a big step in the right direction."

I remember when I traveled, escaping from everyday life. I went to Myrtle Beach, South Carolina. It took a long time to get there. It was summer time and hot, with no A/C in the car. Just myself and the open road.

Once I arrived in SC, I could smell the ocean air, hear the waves beating against the shore. The sea gulls, and warm sand between my feet. There I was with my memories of the past, trying to figure out what I had done wrong. *Why did she hate me so much?* To hear her still ringing in my ears: "You're worthless. You're retarded. You're a whore. You're a bitch. I should have had an abortion when I found out I was pregnant with you." And remembering the beatings and the sexual abuse, asking the little girl inside of me to *please, don't be scared.* Allow the adult to embrace her, to allow her for just once to feel safe.

We had found the place where our healing could begin. A place to enjoy life. The more the waves pounded against the shore line, the louder my cries inside, needing to be released.

Sitting there on the shore I could feel the love from God. It was as if at that moment in time I opened and reopened a very painful experience in my life to allow all the negative emotions to be washed away with the tides, embracing the healing that had begun.

Replacing all the negative words with words of comfort: *You're special. You're not crazy. You deserve to be alive. You can believe in your own dreams.*

At that moment I sprang to life. I laughed for the first time in my life, watching people do silly things. I tasted life. Every day was a brand new day. I enjoyed the summer, having new life given.

I applied to nursing school when I returned home. I started that fall, to prove to myself *I can do this* (3.0 GPA). I became a better mother, friend, wife, daughter.

I forgive all the hurts from yesterday. Those sour bells don't ring in my ears. Only You can exist.

I Am Not Afraid

I am not afraid to be a free thinker.
I am not afraid to say, "No!"
I am not afraid to give my opinion.
I am not afraid to not comb my hair.
I am not afraid to set any kind of goal. And Achieve it!
I am not afraid to do nothing.
I am not afraid to tell someone the truth.
I am not afraid to look someone in the eyes while speaking.
I am not scared of healing from my abuse.
I am not scared to tell someone the truth.
I am not scared to stand on my own two feet.
I am not scared that everyone won't like me.
I am not scared to tell you, "No!"
I'm not afraid to tell someone my needs.

I am not afraid to be loved.
I am not afraid of things that are out of my control.
I am not afraid to look in the mirror and not see any bruises.
I am not afraid to be afraid.
Nor am I afraid to be me.
I am not afraid of failure.
I am not afraid of asking for help.
I am not afraid to tell you to shut up.
I am not afraid to be alone.
I am not afraid to set out to achieve what I set out to achieve.
I am afraid of spiders.

You Cannot Live in My Head

YOU HAVE BEEN EVICTED FROM my life. You can no longer steal my joys, my happiness. You can't live anywhere in my life rent free. I've taken myself back. I belong to the King of Kings, and I won't give in to the spirit of you.

Many nights I laid beside you in a bed of lies.

Along with my Lord Jesus, we reclaim my life. Vanish whence you came. You cannot live in my head. You cannot live any place in my heart. You cannot live any place where I reside.

Before you I was an injured bird. After you I soar with the eagles. Before you I was small and felt like I never mattered. After you, I matter!

Fear, you are plain removed. It's time you live in your own shadow. Back down in your own shadow. Fear begets fear.

MI SUEÑO

Ms. K

Translated by Emily Polanco

DESDE NIÑA HE SOÑADO CON ayudar a las personas, y conforme el tiempo fue pasando venian a mi mente muchas ideas y planes por hacer; por ejemplo: Fui a estudiara Cuba dos años medicina porque quería aprender a cuidar de las personas y sanar sus dolencias físicas como emocionales. No pude concluir allá la carrera pero aprendí mucho acerca del trabajo social y un poco de medicina preventiva. En los siguientes años ya de regreso en mi pais Guatemala comenzaron a surgir deseos por aprender sobre diseño industrial: manufactura de bolsos de mujer, joyas, tarjetas creativas, indumentaria (Ropa, bolsos, zapatos, accesorios). Estaba un poco confundida porque quería seguir estudiando mediana pero a la vez también diseño industrial. Lo que hice fue decidirme por uno de los dos y opté por diseño industrial (claro sin olvidar que mi deso por ayudar a las personas era primordial y relevante). Bueno, entonces comencé a investigar en donde se podía estudiar esa carrera y descubrí que la única Universidad hasta donde yo sabía que daba esa carrera era pagada y bastante costosa. No me desanimé al contrario eso me dio más fuerzas para continuar hasta lograr mi cometido. Con el tiempo empezaron a surgir más y más ideas de como involucrar mi gran deseo de ayudar a las personas sin dejar mi pasión que es el "arte" el cual lo descubrí por medio del diseño industrial. Cerca de mi cama Yo podia ver la necesidad de las personas desde emocional, física, cómo económica. Era un blanco perfecto para involucrarlas en mi "sueño" y poderlas ayudar. Primero comencé elaborando joyas y bolsos de cuero con tela típica de mi país con madera y cobre. Y busqué donde vederlos. Pues dá la causalidad no "casualidad" que me dirigí al Ministerio de Finanzas y Economía de mi país para pedir ayuda por ejemplo un préstamo monetario para iniciar una micro-empresa y aunque no obtuve el préstamo sí un espacio de un kiosko en la Universidad donde podía estudiar diseño industrial. ¡Es maravilloso! Y pues nada, comencé a comercializar mis productos el día del kiosko en el cuál las ganancias qu obtuve sirvieron para reinvertir y producir más.

Ya con esto, comencé a querer mejorar los productos tanta joyas como bolsos de mujer y busqué un orfebre (persona que trabaja con oro y plata) y un ingeniero industrial. Ambos me ayudaron con respecto a mejorar mis productos pero no estaba conforme, necesitaba saber de finanzas personales, negocios, y de como comercializarlos. Busqué en mi iglesia ayuda con respecto a estos ítems y la conseguí. El vice presidente de un banco del sistema me dio consultas de finanzas además trabajo. El escribió un libro referente a finanzas personales. Mi trabajo consistía en buscar lugares adonde se puderian hacer seminarios y vender los libros. De toda la venta del día recibía el cincuenta por ciento. Era algo muy Bueno. Con todo esto na había encontrado cómo involucrar a esas mujeres necesitadas para apoyarlas. Pero el tiempo pasó y decidí de una vez por todas apoyarlas y ¿Cómo fue eso? Ellas íban a manufacturar los productos a íban a tener un salario por su trabajo. Pero ésto conllevaba buscar un lugar y una microfinanciación para la adquisición de material de trabajo. Algo que no quiero dejar pasar por alto es de tallar cuál es mi plan de ayuda para esas mujeres ya que en un futuro lo lograré. Uno de ellos es:

- Capacitación intensive para que los artículos sean de primera calidad.
- Educarlas, qu puedar estudiar si no han terminado su escolaridad.
- Tener terapias psicológicas con cada una de ellas
- Capacitación en finanzas personales
- Plan de ejercicio físico
- Buscarles ayuda conforme sus necesidades
- Entre otras.
- Tengo planes a corto, mediano y largo plazo para llegar y alcanzar ese sueño.
- Todo ésto lo pongo en las manos de Dios, Jesucristo es todo para mí. Por eso no me afano, descanso en la fe en Dios. ¡Amo a Dios!

My Dream

SINCE I WAS A CHILD, I have dreamed about helping other people, and as time passed, I had many ideas and plans for how to do that. For example, I went to study medicine for two years in Cuba because I wanted to learn to take care of people and heal their physical and emotional illnesses. I couldn't make my career there, but I learned a lot about social work and a little about preventive medicine. In the following years I returned to my country, Guatemala. I began to have the desire to learn about industrial design: manufacturing of women's purses, jewelry, creative cards, attire (clothing, purses, shoes, and accessories). I was a little confused because I wanted to continue studying medicine, but also industrial design. I decided I had to choose between the two, and I opted for industrial design (of course, not forgetting that my desire to help others was most important).

Well, then I began to investigate where I could study this career, and I discovered the only university offering this course of study was not free; in fact, it was quite expensive. I didn't get discouraged; in fact, that gave me more ambition to continue to work on achieving my goal.

With time, I had more and more ideas of how to make my big wish to help others come to fruition without leaving behind my passion of art, which I discovered through industrial design. I could see the needs of people from an emotional, physical, and economic standpoint. It was ideal to involve them in my dream, and I could help them. First, I began to develop jewelry and leather purses with traditional Guatemalan fabric, wood, and copper. And I looked for places to sell them. By fate, I was directed to the Ministry of Finance and Economics to ask for help for a loan to begin my own business. I didn't get the entire loan, but enough to have a small space for a kiosk at the University, where I could sell my products. I used the profits to reinvest in what was produced, and to improve the items. I worked with a metalsmith and a designer to create jewelry and handbags. I still needed to learn about the business and financial aspects, and how to market the products. I looked to my church for help, and a vice president from a bank who attended consulted with me about the financial work. He helped me track progress. Wholesale was fifty percent profit, which was very good. I wanted to involve women, to help them support themselves by manufacturing the products so they would be paid for their work. I want to help women in the future. Some of my goals:

- Offer training to create the best quality items.
- Provide access to education for those who haven't finished school.
- Provide therapy
- Financial advice
- Access to exercise
- Finding help for other types of support.
- My goals are short, medium, and long term, but I hope to achieve this dream. I put everything in God's hands. Jesus Christ is everything to me. I don't worry too much, but rest my faith in God. I love God!

WHAT HAVE I LOST?

Ms. K

I LOST MY SECURITY, IDENTITY, home, city, and my personal space. Freedom. Myself.

After I was raped, my entire way of thinking and living changed. I needed to rely on something, someone, other than myself. All I had left was my name, son, DOB, and SSN. And, of course, my God. I hated how I felt. I hated not knowing my path, my direction on my journey. I simply did not know what to do. That's when I dropped to my knees and asked God to guide me, help me focus my anger to seek justice. As I look back, I see all that I found: freedom, peace within my anger because that flame had turned white from red. I see everything that I have learned, good and bad, was for my benefit. My glass is now half-full.

Of course I didn't have all, or most, of the answers. But now I understand that my steps are for a bigger journey. But in the beginning I didn't really understand. Once I was left with the basics, the barest me, I had no choice but to change with the moment, swing with every mood and emotion I felt. Anger became my comfort, my motivator, my friend. My biggest battle was not the judicial system or the levels of government from Chicago, IL to Washington, D.C that had failed my son and I. I was my battlefield. Still, to this day, they can't and won't defeat me. I am the only one with power over me. At least that's what I pray to God for—the strength to win this war. To survive and still be me.

A day in my life is never a dull moment. I never know what is coming. It's always like a freight train full speed ahead, with the stream of anger always close by.

I ask every day for the strength to handle it. I ask for the balance to be my backbone so I don't tip over. Being on the edge normally isn't where people want to be, but for me it's falling into the abyss that worries me. Once you're in there's no coming back. I survive on the edge. It lets me know I'm alive. My anger and my light keep me on the edge like the tip of a sharp, cold sword. Always ready for battle.

Drama

THE ONLY TIME THERE IS no drama is when everyone is on quiet time, 12 AM-6 AM. That is my favorite time of each day. My mind slows down in my space, I can breathe easy and process what has worked my last nerve in the day.

I've made it clear in the morning, I'm a shark in murky water, looking for my first prey of the day. As I head to the bathroom, I'm already thinking, "Who's going to be first?"

Why every single morning must we go to that place? Is that the distraction for the day?

Things To-Do List:

1. Move into my own space (no sharing of the bathroom space!)
2. Don't want to know my neighbors/ Blend in
3. Locate dog park
4. Where are security entrances/exits

5. Safety route
6. Pack a safe bag & have a plan
7. Allow my son to adjust
8. Hot bath—soak these JC months away

Neko/Nikita

A DAY IN THE LIFE of my precious Neko & Nikita—I wonder, if they could talk, what would they say? It's those looks that melt even my walls of steel. Our day starts with a "Good morning." They are the only ones I really want to talk to, besides my son. With tails wagging, collars, kisses, and a poop bag—who could ask for more?

They trot to the elevator looking at everyone looking at them. To keep them focused, I talk to them the whole time. Neko has figured out where to stand on the elevator so the doors will close. Nikita can't wait to get past the doors to the green cool grass. She loves to kick stand in the morning. Neko has a torn ACL, which has really slowed him down. That's probably a good thing. No one has any idea how manic he really is. But I always get asked: do they bite? Lucky for me, a treat is our best motivator. I just can't imagine life without my babies, my family, my service dogs.

IF I WAS A BIRD

Ms. L

I like the way birds soar
high in the sky so freely. So
gracefully. And at the same time
survivors. The bird survives off
the fruits of the land, and is one
of the most vulnerable animals
overall. Birds are one of the easiest
prey in a sense, but at the same
time survivors. In the winter months
they have the strength to fly to
a climate in which they can maintain.
For housing they work diligently to
make a nest for their
family and protect their babies,
like humans, until the egg is ready
to open. A bird's wing can break
but for some reason or way
the bird heals itself and still
soars above all other creations

of God. Not to mention the birds are
very beautiful and humble creatures.
Humble to the notion that they will
accept food from any source and
they will accept help without giving up a fight.

THE STREETS

Ms. M

As a young child I always wanted to be grown. I remember when my mother moved us out of the projects and to a better neighborhood because she wanted a better life, not just for her, but us, her kids, too There are five of us, and of course, I was the bad child.

I remember I met this girl. She was experienced, but I didn't know. I just thought I had made a real friend. We would skip school. She would call dudes over. That's when my life took a turn. I began to sneak out of windows. I went days and nights without going home.

I was twelve years old, and her house was the hang-out spot because her mom was always at work. We also hung out in a place they called "Downtown Dayton." When I look back, I really became somebody I wasn't trying to be. I would be down there fighting and jumping people, being a follower, which led me to the Juvenile Detention Center. From there I just really went wild. I didn't care anymore.

I didn't realize I was hurting people close to me, like my mother and stepdad, my sisters, and brother. They were worried about me. They would always ask me, "Would you just come back?"

Sometimes I would, if food or clothes got low for me or something bad happened to me. After my need was met, I went right back to the streets, which never loved me like I thought.

Here I am, thirty years old, almost headed down that yellow brick road. Out late hours of the night, drinking and going out. I wasn't paying attention to what matters the most to me: my four handsome kids. Instead I was pleasing what was most displeasing in my life: a low-life, weak-minded man. A boy, really. I was weak, and it had hindered my life.

I remember times when my kids would beg me to stay home. Being addicted to the streets, I heard them speak, but didn't listen.

What I lost doing all these things was my mind, my home, my peace. I took my kids' joy away. They almost looked different to me. The only thing I didn't lose was the four of them. They were all I had left after everything was said and done. And for that, I thank God.

There comes a time in your life when you really have to keep it real with yourself, and writing this is where I am beginning my healing process, and realizing where I was wrong. A lot of things happened that my kids didn't deserve. Because I wasn't responsible enough, our power was shut off, dead smack in winter, the week before Christmas. It cost a lot to get it put back on, and I had been going through so much with my ex's abuse, and feeling used. I abused and soaked my feelings with a drink, and once I started it was hard to stop.

I made up my mind that something had to change. My children and I moved to Indianapolis, where my cousin stayed. She had a townhome she wasn't using. That was really a challenge; we walked into a mess. The person who lived there before left the place a big mess. My kids and I teamed up and made the place the best we could. There was power, but no water. But, I could tell my kids were a bit happier. They are brave, I tell you, because of the things we had to do. I don't know if I could have survived what they had to go through: using buckets or cups to use the restroom, and sometimes it was so cold at night we all had to huddle together to stay warm. To see their strength made me realize how I needed to get my life all the way in order.

But just when I tried, my life took a turn I never expected, and as it did, my mind began to replay my mother's voice in my head, saying "You gotta be careful of what you say."

As my mind continued to replay, I heard myself saying the words, "I will never live in a shelter." Yet, here I am.

I remember the night my kids and I packed the car to go. They were all in the car crying and saying they didn't want to go. They cried until the point I almost lost it. But, I gained control, because I knew I had to do what was best. And I did.

The first night was hard, and different, because we had never been through anything like it. In my thirteen years of being a mother, I always was good about keeping a roof and a car provided for my family. There were times I wanted to give up, but I wouldn't allow myself to. So I kept driving to the shelter.

I remember going in and doing the intake, and I just broke down. The woman on staff was very understanding. She made my kids feel a bit more at ease when she explained to them how it works and that we would have our own room, and then she fed us some snacks.

WHAT I HAVE LOST

Ms. N

What I have lost is beyond what anyone could fathom.
It would be easier to jot down what I haven't lost,
but that would be too easy.

What I have lost is the man that was supposed to be my guidance,
support, and shoulder. My father.

What I have lost is the innocence I never got to have, that was
stolen from me. Human trafficking.

What I have lost is the hope and faith of protection
coming to this country. Being raped by police officers.

What I have lost is the chance to be loved because he took control
of my existence. I've lost my daughter from enduring his abuse.

I have lost all the trust in myself,
but I have found that I can gain my childhood through my son

and future baby girl. I have found
that not every man is out to hurt me.

I have now realized that my trust and love can be taken back.
In all the things I've lost and that were taken from me,
I have gained and found twice as much.

I Remember

I REMEMBER SITTING ON THE cold kitchen countertop, five and a half months pregnant with my angel. He yelled, and all I could think was to protect her. I remember my first love—the one who was to protect me, our kids, and my heart—slowly taking my world from me. He dragged me by the hair through the halls. I felt her kicking so hard, but I had no control. He kicked, punched, and slammed my body everywhere. I remember when he was done he spit on me and walked off. I felt wetness, warm and cold, surrounding me. It was my water and blood. I don't remember after that besides seeing her tiny beautiful face. I remember every detail from her small nose, big brown eyes, but the most painful was the tubes connecting to her body. I hate to remember losing her. She was my world and beyond. I remember how angry and hateful I was. I didn't want to eat or shower or even to live anymore. I'll always remember her eyes, her tiny fingers gripping mine. I remember I never wanted to let go.

WHAT HAVE I LOST?

Ms. N

MY KIDS. NOWHERE TO STAY.
My mother passed away. Family don't care.
Been in and out of domestic abuse all my life.
I been by myself with no help all my life.

I was in Saginaw, MI. I lost the kids due to domestic violence. There was no support. My sister got custody of two of my kids. I have five kids from ages twelve to twenty-one. The twelve year-old and sixteen year-old are with my sister.

In Saginaw on Warren St. in an apartment. When I was pregnant, he shot at me seven times. God protected me.

He also jumped on me real bad. Every time he jumped on me, he broke my nose, he busted both my eyes.

I stayed at the Underground Railroad Saginaw, a shelter. I escaped and went out of town, but I went back, and I was bound.

I'm sad a lot, but you'd never know it. My eighteen year-old had a heart condition, open heart surgery as an infant. We were reunited in 2015 in July—she looked me up on the Internet and sent a friend request. We have only talked on the phone. The last time I saw her, she was as a baby.

I remember when one daughter was taken from me as a baby. She found me eight months ago, and we still have not seen each other.

I woke up in the middle of the night to a message, and I thought: Wow, she looks just like my son. I stared at the picture for an hour, but I knew it was her. I wrote, "I have a daughter named ____. Is that you?" She sent me back all the birth information from her document. I said, "Oh, my gosh, that is you."

She went to prom this year, graduated—but I don't get to see it. I lost her as an infant because of him. He would jump on me all the time—police had to guard my hospital room.

We talk and text every day, but I've never seen her.

I remember when my family turned their back on me. I remember when I went back to Detroit, MI with nowhere to go and asked my sister if I could stay with her and my kids until I got myself together, and she put me out of her house with nowhere to go. I remember when my sixteen year-old cried to go with me, and I could not take her 'cause I lost all my rights with her due to her dad taking her to another state, and he told the courts that he didn't know where I was at.

When she was with her dad for visitation, he took her out of state to Alabama, and took away my rights to see her. She was only supposed to go to his house for the weekend.

THE LOVINGS' FAMILY VALUES

Quindara Lovings

I REMEMBER SOUNDS OF LAUGHTER. Crying children, family cheering when me and my kids arrive at family events. I remember balloons popping, bounce houses, splashing of water, sounds of love. Smells of cotton candy, flavored popsicles and Grandmother's perfume. Budweiser from my mother's coffee cup, and Wild Irish Rose lingering from my father. I smell marinated and dry-rubbed meat on the grill. Corn, the smell of flowers, fresh cut grass—always making me sneeze because of allergies. Scent of innocence coming from a newborn. The smell of breast milk coming from my brother's mouth when I put him to bed after feeding him a bowl of corn flakes. My brother tricked me and dumped water all over me. I waited until years later for revenge. I asked the doctor, what made the baby go to sleep with breast milk?

I waited until my brother had a hot date. He always wanted to eat cereal.

Growing up I saw violence. I heard the sounds of fighting. Lies, betrayal, rules. Rules that were being taught, but never practiced by the teachers. Speeches of love, and familiness, and standing together—but never put into action.

Promises broken. Poor examples of parenting. But I saw that one lost piece of gold in the mine: children. Born into nothing.

Lost hopes and dreams, no ambition, and no faith to turn out to be something no one would ever imagine. Some of the bravest, strongest kids: nieces, nephews, brothers, and sisters that have done great things, accomplished more than expected. And some are still destined to do great things.

Now I am a grown woman, big sister, role model, and mother.

I see the heavy-drinking and poly-drug use. I see him passed out on the couch or drunk, asleep in the car with it still running. I see my mom passed out behind crack houses.

I see life support numbers racing up and down all night, tears rolling down the faces of her children, left behind. All the while wondering, *How am I gonna take her place?* And raise three kids— and one still left to find.

On top of raising my own four seedlings, trying to encourage them and enforce strength, promote non-violence, no fighting amongst the four strangers, not including myself.

How to teach them to come together as brothers and sisters. How to forgive, hearing the sound of your sibling. Say I love you. And I forgive you. Making them appreciate and understand the smell of their own blood. Trying to teach them patience when you already have a low tolerance for stupidity, for excuses. To prepare them for what's ahead when their mother dies after two years in hospice, after only being promised six months due to the drinking and drug use which she chose for twenty-seven years.

At just fifty-three a beautiful life and woman was lost. Rita Lovings will forever be missed.

Even with the drug use, the abandonment, the violence, the hitting, disrespect, the attempts to push away love that you really needed, the hatred and the slander, talked about from others, never stopped me from searching for you, yearning for you, needing stories from you directly instead of someone else. From a child until now I still love you and forgive you, and I would trade my life for yours. I didn't know you long, but from 2012 until now, I appreciate.

The party's over. Street lights are on. Time to come into the house. What you couldn't do from earth—maybe God can teach you to be the best mother you can be, from Heaven.

As a young girl growing up and learning all the bad—backstabbing lies, betrayal, molestation, torture, abuse, seeing and hearing domestic violence like a bedtime story set off every night, like an alarm clock of drunken behavior. To be shown and to learn all the bad things in the world.

To have seen and known nine relationships, and not ever shown a real stepmother. To see what it was to hurt someone, to use someone and their children. To see disrespect from your "superhero," the parent that did step up when drug addict mother gave up. To love a man you remember seeing hurt women, drink gallons every day, and who took his anger out on you when the ladies in his life upset him.

To grow up knowing that some of your attackers were your own father's friends.

That you could have been a drug sale.

To never know the answers is a lot to hold onto. But, there is a blessing—and the blessing is that you learn all the bad things in the world. Every single one. There's nothing left to learn but the good.

And, you develop a defense mechanism: to turn every single one of those bad things into something positive. To smile. To laugh. So you don't grow up bitter. So you don't grow up weak. So you can give that one little girl or boy who has nothing something to look up to. To have them love. Trust, forgive. Unconditionally love each other.

I was blessed from one of the stepmothers who might have been the Devil's advocate, but she had a true God as her friend. She came around when I was about nine years old, and put music back into my heart, rhythm in my step, that bass in my soul. She stopped my last suicide attempt.

I was a little backwards as a kid. I used to let six girls jump me every day. I tried to hang myself in the bathroom in the third grade. I've overdosed. I took pop cans to slice up my arms. That's just from ages six to ten. I wanted the pain to stop. I wanted my dreams to be reality.

All that time, there was a reason God wouldn't let me go. He used her to make me understand I don't have to be like my parents. I could find the positive. There is someone with heart, that stepped up and saved one girl's heart from suicide. She came into my life as a woman I could grow into, to give me a chance. Without her helping me through the war, I don't know where I'd be. Her and God.

Every child needs a role model—if not that, then someone talking plain common sense to them. She always kept telling me there's always someone out there that has it worse, but you have to fight, and live for today, "Because joy comes in the morning." She said that a lot. I believed her for a while. But my life kept hitting the rewind button.

I know the story seems pretty bad, and that's only a tiny part of it. It's about bad parenting.

I'm a mother of four. My parents taught me what a mother is *not*. What a parent is *not*. What kind of husband I *don't* want and how a lady *shouldn't* carry herself. I thank them for that. Not a lot of people learn all the mistakes first. When you learn all the mistakes first it can only make a better you. Things you never want your children to live, feel, encounter. Having this kind of upbringing can protect them eighty percent more than a two-parent home.

As a mom I am overprotective, even from their father. In my neighborhood, sometimes you can't even trust a father, cousin, uncle. In our household, a few things to learn: little girls never sit on laps, and if they do, it is only on the knee area, no kissing little girls on the mouth, do as told when told, keep shirt and dresses down, no flipping or twirling or lifting dress or shirt when men are around. Men stay in one room, and the women and children are separate. Even wives don't sit with the men while they're smoking.

We keep our children in the kitchen young, not because we are too lazy to cook, but in case Mom or Dad passes out—then you can still survive.

When the police come, the kids hide until they leave. Have to hustle and panhandle to take care of the kids while the parents are gone. My cousins steal or rob from tourists or out-of-towners because they're hungry. Sometimes they rob because they're angry. Sometimes they rob and throw the money away because they think it's funny.

In this family, children stick together.

We had a few uncles that taught us sayings to live by. One was bitter from the war, and since his wife died. "Find 'em, Fuck 'em and Forget 'em. That way you'll never get hurt." That's what he taught the boys and me. "No need to cry over spilt milk. You already knew it was destined to happen." "In the Bible, God says you can't trust men."

I see the women in my family cry and break down, and then run back to the man beating them and calling them names. They lost my respect—teaching us to accept it and teaching brothers that it's OK.

If you need to cuss at a spouse, that's not love. If you think God gives you the right to discipline your spouse, that's not love. If you embarrass your spouse and chastise them in the family or out in public, that's not love.

People don't know. Love is love. It doesn't hurt. It's supposed to make you feel good, like Kenny G on the radio, or Sade in the breeze, Mays blazin' out "Joy & Pain."

Even when someone passes away and you blurt out, "Man, I loved them!" That doesn't hurt, you feel good in that moment. Hurt is missing them and not hearing their voice.

A scar or bruise can hurt because every time you look at it you see what you heard and what you felt when you got it. Sorry is a hurt. It means nothing. Just words. Truly apologizing from the heart is showing improvement, not just talk.

I don't entertain bullshit. I have friends with six or seven kids, married to drug dealers—men who do nothing to impress me. My friends envy me.

They ask:

How do I get someone to care for me?

How do I get up and move out of state with nothing?

How do I take care of these kids with no job?

Why smile when your father beat you almost to death?

How do you laugh when your mother's life is in the balance?

Or why walk two miles with twine to move furniture?

How do you face one last baby getting a blood transfusion and almost dying on the table?

Then you're not thinking about yourself but reminding people of what they need to get up and do.

When I had a baby, when he died—if God takes him, then they are just on loan to see how we're going to take care of them. So I can never be mad because God needed him more than I did.

A couple years later I birthed a son. I knew he was guaranteed to do great things because at this point, I knew my worth with God, not with society. No more thoughts of suicide. I had a new job now, and a second chance at being a Mom, the greatest job on earth. You have to be highly trained in all fields: first teacher, counselor, chef, plumber, everything. Most first-time parents are scared to death because they have no idea what to do. When you learn what not to do, then you get it right.

The minute that baby cried I jumped up and I said, "Hey, I've been waiting for you to wake up!" Excitement, the rhythm beating. Finally, something that's all mine.

In late summer 2004, my best friend said she was moving to Indianapolis (she had eight sisters). I had nine friends I hung out with in school. I had the first baby of them all.

I was mother, nurturer, the bossy one. I was the friend who would never let you drive drunk. I'll punch you in the face to keep the keys.

If you are fighting and drunk, I will take your kids and keep them for the night. You can get them in the morning. Kids don't need to listen to the song of fighting every night.

When I die, whether people hate me or love me, they'll always say I told the truth. I'm the friend who was never afraid to say what's true.

I had one friend who smelled so bad everyone complained about her stinking up their cars, furniture, place. I defended her, "You don't know what her story is. She's our friend, and you don't even know if her mom ever taught her how to take care of herself." Maybe her mom wasn't a mom, like mine.

We were all at a picnic and I said to her, "So, do you need some clothes? I have some in my car. Do you need a toothbrush? Soap? My Auntie lives down the street if you need a shower. Because, you do have an odor, and if I have to hear anyone mention it, I'm going to jail."

She was mad for a long time, but she did get over it. Then, when she saw me again, she got on her knees, and she said, "It was horrible, these weeks without you."

In my mind, as a friend, male or female, you're not a friend unless you're helping with life. I don't care about weed, drinks, bars, guys.

Let's teach each other to be stronger, to be better women, wives, husbands. Let's teach our daughters not to settle for less, and not to settle for just anything. Let's teach our sons to be productive, to be gentlemen, and men in society. But, you have to catch the kids young. When they're one, two, or three.

I never had the "terribles." Instead of buying nerf guns and super-slides, in our home you get them a kitchenette set with a broom and dust pan—not as a toy, to use it. When you mop, hand them a mop, too. Be more involved with your children. It starts when they're young, just like early reading. Be consistent with the child.

My twins think laundry day is like going to Chuckie Cheese. I can't just say, "Put this in the wash," I have to give them jobs because they will fist fight for who helps Mom first. They used to fight right on my lap.

Take the clothes from the dryer, dump the basket like diving on a pile of leaves, diving for socks and underwear.

As they get older and become teenagers, with attitudes, I won't have such a problem—explaining to them young, why they have to do this every day. They will learn to be independent. They will know how to take care of themselves. This is a way to stop petty fights and not feel dependent on someone all the time.

If it's for family, we're running whenever they call, no matter what they need. Outsiders have to work harder.

When my kids fight, when I feel unappreciated even from a six-year-old, I tell them, "Our last name is Loving. We are the Lovings family. It's not OK to treat each other that way." I say that, because I'm going to be the one to break this generational curse.

When sisters, cousins, or nieces get a boyfriend it won't be the father sitting down with him, it will be me.

You will not come in and cause them added stress or heartache.

If anyone wants to date these little ones and isn't a soother and a problem solver, isn't calm in the morning, then get thee behind me! You get a zero, just like the devil. People forget that he is under our feet, and we walk over him every day. They're just mind games, to test you.

Even when under stress, you still win when God wakes you up that next morning.

But we, me and my best friend, her older sister brought us here to come stay with her boyfriend. Like a cliché—three women in a house with one man, something went wrong.

He kept hitting on my friend and sent her home. I wasn't going back home with my new baby. My baby had lots of fevers. We were at the hospital more than three times in less than three months.

At the last hospital trip, the nurse didn't care for blacks much. I heard her comments to the staff and other nurses when she came in for the late shift.

The doctor and the other nurse had said I would need to sign a waiver to put my baby in a cab with their car seat. They said, "Bring the seat back in two days or we will charge you $50.00."

The other nurse was late. I told her I already watched the car seat video. I went to the bathroom, and she snooped in my purse. She saw a bottle of depression medicine from my doctor in Kalamazoo. When my baby was only one month old he prescribed them and said, "If you feel depressed then take them to ward off postpartum." He said take them if I need them, and if I don't, then don't.

She thought something of it because there were only two pills missing from the bottle of thirty. The previous nurse had already signed the discharge form. I went to smoke. I watched the car seat video again. She asked for $50.00 and I told her about what the doctor said. I was on the phone, and asked her to bring the car seat. The nurse said she was calling the doctor to see if I was telling the truth.

It was taking forever. The person on my phone says, go look for the nurse. I found her crouched down, telling someone on the phone my son's name, date of birth, address, my name.

I decided to scare her, because I'm funny, "Hey, who are you talking to?"

She said, "The mom is right here."

I got on the phone and they lied. They said they weren't going to take my baby. They said that the man I was living with was accused of statutory rape.

I wasn't sleeping with him. We met at church, and he said he would wait for me.

They said they were coming to give me paperwork. They came in with two sheriffs.

They said they were concerned that my baby had been in the hospital with reflex disorder more than three times. I was seventeen. They said they were taking my baby to a hospital for babies with this disease and that he would have to stay there, or he could die.

So, I signed everything they told me to sign. And then they made me a ward of the state.

They told my fiancé they would arrest him for kidnapping and statutory rape. He said he didn't know me because they had him scared, and believing that he would go to jail.

They took me to a "hospital" off of Washington St. The Guardian Home. They left me in the lobby with my portable DVD player, my cell phone, and whatever I had brought with me to the hospital.

They said my baby would be coming through the double doors. They said, "You'll see your baby." I'm waiting three days. No baby. Just waiting.

They say they don't know anything. They told me I could have lunch in the cafeteria. I ask the desk if I can call the hospital. I ask, "Who can help us?" Since she keeps saying no one can help.

I jump over the counter, "Call the hospital! Say who I am, ask what's going on. I just want to know, where's my baby?"

They tell me no one with that name is at the hospital. I say, "Oh, so you're kidnapping kids down here?" I went crazy. I said, "Find someone from the hospital to talk to me right now." I don't even see people coming in and out of the double doors.

She says, "I wasn't here when you came."

I said, "I know my baby's hungry."

She said, "Who brought you here?" She called someone.

Lunch time comes around. The lady taps me on the shoulder and says I have a phone call.

"Hi, Miss Lovings."

"Are you going to tell me about my baby? Who are you?"

"Yes, we have your kid. Here's what's going on: Your kid is a ward of the state. Here in Indiana you can't be under eighteen, without a parent, and have a baby."

In Michigan I had everything. You have a kid, you become an adult. I said, "I'm at this hospital."

She said, "Not a hospital. We are going to place your baby there, but we are too afraid you're going to run."

I'm getting angry, thinking that she was talking about track and field. In my head all I hear is *Kidnapped. I'm on the phone with the kidnapper.* And I'm going off on the phone; I ask about breast feeding, I have no pump. My breasts hurt.

"What are you feeding him? Tell me where he is so I can see my baby."

"I can't because you're a ward of the state."

I said some crazy shit, "I'll come out with some moves Bruce Lee doesn't even know! I will chop your body up into fifty pieces!"

Threatening was not working. I walked out. Then they put out a missing persons report, a runaway alert, and said they would charge me with neglect and child abuse if I didn't come back.

I went back. I asked for my baby, "I don't know if he's dead or not. If you killed him at the hospital. I'm going nuts."

I went to the bathroom to relieve myself of the milk. A staff member saw me and said I was acting out sexually.

They put me in this cell of a room. They gave me a notebook, and I wrote how I would kill them. I took the wire from the notebook and put it around my neck, threatened to kill myself if I didn't have my baby.

They called my family and talked to my aunt. They never talked to my father. They couldn't talk to my mother because she's a drug addict.

They took my cell phone. They moved me in the middle of the night, putting a pillow case over my head.

I had only two or three months until I turned eighteen. They kept saying that at eighteen I could have my baby back. But the paperwork was all wrong, and the dates were wrong. Because I threatened suicide and violence, they kept me as a ward of the state past eighteen. They said I was a danger.

How I Got Here

I LOST THE CAR, WENT to jail. My mother died. Stepmother died. Stepfather died. My kids were moved into another foster care home. My twins have been beaten and raped since being taken out of my care.

Walking from the Convention Center I was attacked, raped, kidnapped. I came to the Julian Center.

HE WASN'T GOOD FOR ME

Ms. S

I CAME HERE IN 2014 from New York. My ex-husband's relatives in Indianapolis called me to come to them. We were already separated at the time, but they wanted me to come here because he was here. My ex-husband's cousins came to drive me here from New York.

My ex-husband wanted me back, but he wasn't good for me. He didn't trust me. If I was going somewhere, he would call me while I was asleep. Whenever I didn't answer the phone, he would think I was going out somewhere. I would be calling my mother in India and he would tell me not to talk with her. He would fight with me so often in Indiana.

One day, March 19th, my daughter had a fever of 103 degrees, and I called my husband to come back because she wasn't okay. He said he was coming, and I brought her to his brother's house and gave her medicine. I called the doctor, who told me to go to the ER. My neighbor stopped by and told me to go to the ER. I didn't have a car at the time, so I didn't know how to go to the hospital. She called her brother and his friend, who took us to the ER. My friend's friend helped me to talk to the doctors; my English is weak. My husband was calling me, but I was busy at the hospital. He didn't meet me until three hours later. My friend and her male friend stayed with me, and he was upset that I was with a boy. He accused the friend of being my boyfriend. I asked him to stop and go home—allow me to explain later—but he insisted that he was my boyfriend. He called me names at the hospital in front of everyone. He insisted that we were together, asking for my phone. But I refused to hand it over. We had been there for five hours when my husband's brother showed up at the hospital to gossip.

The doctor discharged my daughter, and I called my husband to pick us up again and again. But he insisted he was coming for us. When we were home, I was sitting eating bread and beans. He wasn't fighting with me then, but continued to ask about the male friend.

"Who is he?" he asked angrily.

"Her friend," I told him.

"Fine, don't tell me," he replied.

In the morning, he told me he would go to get the medicine for our daughter at the store. He took my phone and my file full of information and deleted all of the photos of us. He had been gone for several hours, and when he was home he gave everything back. But I didn't notice that the photos were erased. He continued to insult me: "You are a prostitute. I don't like you."

"These are my files, my papers." And he opened my file and threw out my information. He started kicking me and pushing me in the back.

I went into the yard, yelling for help. He followed me, grabbing me and pulling me back towards the house. He finally gave up and left, leaving me and my daughter crying.

The apartment wasn't mine; it was his cousin's, owned by his family. His cousin came over into the apartment and said, "Your husband isn't coming back. You have to leave with your daughter."

"I don't have money, and I don't have anywhere to go," I told him.

He says, "You go anywhere. You can go to a friend's house."

I said I would go with my ex-husband.

March 25th, he came back. He told me he had given me the time to leave and didn't understand why I wasn't gone. I told him again how I had no money and nowhere to go. My ex-husband came back and started throwing our stuff out, scaring me. My daughter was sleeping, so I asked him to stop yelling. He continued to loudly talk at me, waking up my daughter who started to cry again.

I asked him to stop and he pushed me. I hit my head on the wall, crying. He continued to throw out my things, scaring both me and my daughter. But he didn't stop.

"You don't stop, you can't—. Stop. I'm going to call the police if you don't stop." He got angry and tore my shirt open down the front with his hands. My daughter was crying in the background.

My daughter came towards me, and I held her to me. I threatened again to call the police. He said, "Do it, call the police. Do it."

He came up and slapped me and my daughter. I didn't know what number to call – 911 or 119 – and it wasn't working. I finally got it right and told them that he was beating me and that he punched me while I was on the phone. He left soon after.

The police showed up at the apartment and took me and my daughter to the hospital. They called an advocate for me and brought me to the Julian Center.

My hearing was on May 25th. The judge said my daughter would get three hours, three days a week of visitation with my husband. Two-year protective orders were given against my ex-husband and his cousin. My husband tries to tell the judge that he wants me – his family – back. My husband accepted the protective order against him under the condition that he gets to see our daughter.

The next hearing is on September 13th, where the protective order will be up for review because of the split custody. The two years may be changed after reviewing how my husband has been with his time with my daughter. The hearings for my husband and his cousins are in two different counties on the same day. In the hearing with my husband, my attorney speaks for me.

I feel better here because the people help me. It is good for me to be here.

My father and my husband's father were friends. My father decided his family was good, and that we should get married. It was an arranged marriage. We had been married three-and-a-half years. We got divorced in 2015 – about a year after. We were married in the states.

I was twenty-two when I moved to the states, and my daughter was born here at St. Francis, Greenwood, IN.

Indian families want boys. My ex-husband's family doesn't treat me well for having a daughter. They are not good for me or my daughter.

When I was doing laundry, he would time me. And ask how much money I was spending and where. I don't understand why he was controlling me so much. He would call constantly, asking where I was and what I was doing. If I was visiting the neighbor, he would tell me to go home – ask me to call him on FaceTime to prove that I was home.

My father lived in Canada, but he passed away. He had been sick for a while, and the doctor told me he didn't have long. He had a brain aneurism while driving and was in the hospital a month before he passed, but I couldn't go see him.

My mother still lives in India. We talk every day. She is worried about me. I don't know why my husband wouldn't trust me to talk with my mother. I'm originally from Punjab, India, where my mother lives. We were always close before I came here. But I won't go back, and haven't been back in three years. I don't know if my mother will visit.

A girl that volunteers at the Julian Center helped me speak and learn English, translating for me. I go to her home sometimes, and her family is very nice. She brings me food because I don't eat chicken; I'm a vegetarian. She comes with me to my hearing dates. She says I am her big sister. She and my daughter get along very well. Her mother buys me and my daughter clothes.

On my first day at the Julian Center, I was scared. I didn't know if it was good for me and my daughter. She is always sick. I'm scared that she is always sick, and I worry about her. She is my life. When she was born, I was sitting in the bed and my husband called his sister who lives in India, and she was the one that picked my daughter's name.

My daughter likes being at the Julian Center because she gets to socialize with the other children. She is very social. When she wakes up in the morning and we go into the dining room, she'll look for people and say hello to everyone. She is happy here. She doesn't like the playroom, though. She likes it when the other kids are there, otherwise she cries. She loves the park. One day, when I went to the park with my friend, we saw the park was closed. My daughter started walking by herself to the park and refused to come back when I told her it was closed; she ran away. Her favorite thing to do at the park is swing on the swing set. She always wants me to be the one to push. I tell her to kiss me, and she'll give me kisses on the cheek. Everyone likes her; she's very friendly. When I go to say something at the front desk, she'll try to copy me and what I'm saying.

I want my daughter to grow up and have a good life and a good job. Maybe a doctor. She is a good person. I want to give her every happiness. I want her to grow up and for people to think that she is a good person. I want to be able to help her go to school and pay for her education. I will work for her to have that life. I want her to grow up with the best education she can get.

LEFT TO WANDER

Ms. S

A T AGE TWELVE I LOST my grandmother. She raised me from the age of five. I loved my grandma with all I have in me. She is the reason I have hope in this messed up world. She is the reason I strive to be a good mother. The reason I never give up. The reason I keep fighting. I remember sitting and curling my grandma's hair for hours, or rubbing Bengay on her back. My time with my grandma was priceless. It's a lot like me and my daughter's time. The love my grandma had for me is the same love I have for my daughter. It's unconditional. The love I have for my daughter is eternal.

I have lived a rough life. Grandma passed away when I was twelve, and I was sent to my mother, whom I had begged for, cried for. My heart ached for a very long time. Once I was finally there, her husband didn't want me. She was an alcoholic and didn't love anyone but herself. She would stay out all hours, and if she wasn't home I wasn't allowed in.

After numerous nights of wandering the streets I knew nothing about, I met a friend. She was my age and her mom spoiled her, bought her everything. I often found myself wishing I was her, since I had to buddy up with the school staff for clothing and shoes. Her mom's love was pure and unconditional and I so badly wanted something like that. Eventually, her mom let me come stay with them so I didn't have to wander the night any longer. Unfortunately, my friend liked to smoke weed, and she liked it a lot. So much she was stealing stuff out of the house and trading it for weed. Who better to blame it on than the house guest, me!

I wanted nothing more than to be trusted, and to fit in. So I began to tell on her before she could blame it on me. Her mom was opening her house to me. I wouldn't dare to steal or take something, and risk being back outside alone and scared.

Eventually, she began to run away with older men. I would stay and try to do as much as possible to remain unseen, fearing her mom would find out she wasn't there and then put me out, too. One day she called and said she was in Chicago and wanted to send me a bus pass to come there. I decided not to. I didn't have a home or anyone who wanted me, but I didn't want the life I knew she was living there.

I called her back a few days later, and she told me she was chained to a hot water heater in a closet and to please help her. I called her mom. Her mom made all kinds of noise until the police busted in on a sex trafficking ring, where she was being held. They brought her back home and she seemed as if she was going to sit still for a while, but no she didn't.

I soon met a new friend. She was nineteen, I was now fifteen, with my permit, and she lived a life filled with drugs, sex, and money in the worst parts of the city. I remember the first time I drove her car to 42nd and Carrolton, we got pulled over and the police pulled us out of the car. They searched everything, everywhere. They even pulled the seats out, confident they were going to find something, drugs, guns, something, but didn't. I was scared to death. I had never been pulled over before, let alone searched that way.

I remember they asked me something and I was speechless. She immediately cut in and answered the question. Then they asked me another question, and I was searching for my words, but I just couldn't find them. She cut in again.

The cop finally said, "Are you stupid or something? Can you talk?"

I muttered, "Yes." I had so much to say, but just couldn't make the words meet my lips.

After leaving, we went to her boyfriend's house. We pulled up in the driveway and saw him go running by us fast, with the cops behind him. My heart dropped to my stomach. No, not again!

My friend said, "Everybody duck down!" So me and the three others all ducked down in our seats. We hadn't fooled anyone because there were the police knocking on my window with a flashlight. I immediately sat up and rolled my window down.

The police said, "You guys again! What are you snow bunnies doing in this area?"

Then all of a sudden I heard a voice say "Them my nieces. They here to get their hair done." I had never been here or even met this lady, but I immediately felt a sense of relief, like I was saved.

• *Art by Stevie Richardson* •

THIS ISN'T THE END FOR ME

Stevie Richardson

Where I'm From...

I HAVE COME FROM TWO people, but they weren't supposed to be together. They were young and they made a mistake and had a baby. My mother was so excited and thrilled, regardless of the obstacles and hardships that would eventually come our way. My mom is always happy and supportive, but my father—well, I can recall on one hand how many times I've seen him happy. A lot of people find him scary, but not me. When I look at him he is translucent: a miserable, selfish, pathetic excuse for a human being. A terrible father, who left. Some of my earliest memories are of him being locked up in his own room, separate from my mom. All he did was work and smoke and play video games. Completely ignoring us all the time. Never having an interest in me. I learned about rejection early because of him. Because he never cared and wasn't like the other dads at my school, the ones who spent time with their kids. Who did homework, ate dinner, and bonded with their kids. I never could understand why he didn't, or didn't want to. How staying in a tiny room by yourself is more enticing than a family dinner, movie, or bonding session. Even though he lived with my mom, he was still a stranger to me. Regardless of how many years he lived with us.

Until I got older, all I wanted was to be left alone. Before they close down, my favorite place used to be Borders Bookstore. Bookstores are the only place I feel free and uninhibited. In between the shelves I feel happy and safe, and like I'm not myself.

I remember when I first realized how much I disappointed my father for not partying or dating young. I kept my focus on school, and he rejected me because I wasn't popular or slutty like his friends' daughters. To him, it was like I wasn't experiencing life. Except that I was experiencing life, just not like a normal teenager.

Being hungry for days at a time and too depressed to care, or having anxiety so bad I had panic attacks just thinking about leaving the house. Having no air in eighty-degree weather taught me more about people and life than getting drunk and going to prom ever could. But some things he'll never know because he never cared to ask.

Maybe there is a reason your teenage daughter is scared to leave the house. But that never crossed your mind, either.

I remember when my dad would give me money each Christmas and birthday, but that was when I confused money for love and attention. There is nothing special or thoughtful in giving someone money so you don't have to deal with them. That all stopped when I turned sixteen years old, before my mother and I were homeless.

I remember on my sixteenth birthday my mom drove me to my dad's house to get my money, and when I walked into his tiny one-bedroom apartment there were pictures of a brand new baby on his walls. I guess he figured that having a baby wasn't important enough to tell his daughter, me. Maybe he thought since I spent my entire life being an only child I would be jealous, or wouldn't want to meet her. It's been four years, and I still don't know her name.

I remember when my dad used me as a pawn to try and get my mom back. But I'm older, and my mom is wiser, so when she made it clear they would never be together he completely ceased the extremely small relationship we barely had at that point.

I remember when my mom and I were homeless and I called him for help and he basically said there is nothing he can do. I remember the next day, we were homeless. He still didn't care. I remember I called him, and I wish I never did. I remember realizing when I got to the Julian Center that my mom's mom and my mom's brother and sister turned their back against us, and from that moment forward they were not family anymore.

I remember breaking my foot, and my father thought we were lying for no reason. All we needed were clothes, because we arrived at the Julian Center with nothing but the clothes on our back. I remember that some of the people at the Julian Center helped and supported us more than some of our ex-family ever did. I remember how shocked I was that people in a shelter that also have nothing were still willing to help us with the very little they had, and no ulterior motives. I'm grateful that I realized even family members can be toxic and need to be let go.

I remember when I realized during art therapy at the Julian Center that I am only nineteen, and this isn't the end for me. Opportunities are endless for someone my age, and I can't let my dad and my family's negative energy hold me back from reaching my greatest potential.

I have to remember that my foot will heal, and because of all the bad things I've been through, someday I'll be able to help someone else because I have been through it all.

Outside of Me / Inside of Me

MY FATHER IS CONCRETE BEING drilled, and my mom is a gardener, and I am a flower she's constantly watering in hopes that I grow. I am constantly reminded that I am not a weed stuck in the sidewalk crying for sunlight and rain—and I never will be.

I remember being bitter and sad that I would never get the chance to be a big sister and that I was denied the opportunity, but now I accept it. My only hope is that he is a better father to her than he ever was to me—that he properly learns to love his child and the best way to express that.

Outside of me is filled with positive, helpful people for the most part. Or maybe people are so helpful because my foot is broken and I'm in a wheelchair, so they take pity on me, though this situation isn't permanent, and I don't need pity.

Outside of me, everything is put together and clean and organized. Inside of me, it is the complete opposite. Inside of me, my insecurities lurk, my dreams and ambitions swirl in my head, and my fears paralyze me. Inside of me, anxiety and depression freeze and control my every move until I don't feel like myself and can't speak to people or organize my thoughts. My anxiety and depression overpower me until I feel like they're my boss, and I'm their robot. Sometimes it makes me feel like I am not even a person, but I am two things: anxiety and depression.

Letter to My Father on My Twentieth Birthday

AT THE AGE OF EIGHT, I realized you weren't so great. At ten, I realized how unimportant I was to you. A day before I turn twenty, I am grateful to be much wiser than you. An hour before midnight I must admit that your selfish, demeaning, and greedy ways were not all your fault. It was because of how you were raised.

Born the first day of July at 1:44 p.m., with the sun high and bright. Only Mother Nature could dim her light, shun us away. Nineteen years later I would hope and pray to feel the sun and be as fearless as I was that bright blue summer's day.

Six months old, and already talking before I could walk. Walking, innocently unaware that in ten more years crowds would have me running scared. Something I couldn't stand. Two years earlier, unbeknownst to me, anxiety had clearly staked me as her lifelong best friend. At age eight, I realized you weren't so great. Still blind to my daughterly love as you nitpicked me about my weight.

When I turned ten, it was so crystal clear to me that a father's love does not equate to money, and I couldn't love and respect you as my father. It was just too late. As I got older, my favorite color always having been blue, you breaking my heart so often slowly changed the hue. Whenever I think of my father's face I am reminded of a gray rainy day.

I could see not all wounds are visible because deep down inside his frozen heart, he was just as miserable.

On the day of my sixteenth birthday, everything changed for the good. I went over to his apartment to get my birthday money. He let me inside, and much to my surprise I saw the truth of one of his lies. On his pale white living room walls where my baby pictures once hung were pictures of his secret six-month old baby. Dotting his walls like fixtures, no space. Shocked and stunned, his secret hit me like brick walls. Questions circled my head: how could he hide this from me? My sweet-sixteen birthday was forever taken from me. Once he got his replacement, he made it clear that of all his children I was the one with the most potential wasted. And the most fear. He made it clear how much hate he has for me.

I'm sad to say, regardless of parts of my childhood being the best, you were a negative and miserable man I could never stand.

Best part of all is you thought I wouldn't heal. Because of my mom I am able to feel grateful, and to be less and less like you every day. I pray to be always more like my mom. Having a mother who is the complete opposite of you was my biggest blessing. Having an unemotional, subpar, humorless father like you was the biggest lesson. But thanks to you I've learned what kind of person I should be because of my mom's example, because of her beautiful qualities. I was raised to be free, to be me. With all I've been through, when I think of you it's like going to the restroom.

This man who helped raise me—I spent my entire childhood with him, and he still doesn't know the person I want to be. A day before I am twenty, and my mother says I'm much wiser than he was.

All I ever aimed for was to be free. I'm grateful his genetics do not make all of me, that I am more than his genetic misery.

I REMEMBER

Ms. T

I REMEMBER THAT MAY TO September in 2014 and into 2015 was a difficult time, but God gave me strength.

I remember God is my life, without him I have no life.

I remember God has sent me good people in my life, especially here in U.S.A.

I remember I can't speak English.

I remember I can't understand people's conversations.

I remember I am scared to talk to people and meet people.

I remember my case manager here at the Julian Center offered support and helped me to take classes at Ivy Tech, and now I listen better and can speak with people. She is a very nice woman, and all the Julian Center officers, and case managers, too; they help people. I honestly am glad to be here with them.

I remember I lived for six months, in 2015, in an Alternative Shelter in Anderson. I remember it was at midnight that my friend took me to Indiana, to the place in Anderson, and I was very scared because I was new to the U.S.A. I lived almost three months with my ex-husband in his house and couldn't go outside much and couldn't meet people. That night I couldn't sleep. I was so stressed and I hated myself; I can't explain. It was a very difficult situation, but the shelter manager and other case managers were very nice and treated me so well. I remember I could hardly eat the food, and I had a coffee addiction, and was so stressed.

I can't sleep or dream, and I spend a lot of time alone. I go to a psychiatrist. It doesn't help me. They gave me sleeping medicine. I used it, but it's no help. I remember one day I cried to God. He is hearing me and answers me. I hear God speak, and listening to preaching makes me feel better. But at this difficult time the Shelter people are with me.

I'M NOT AFRAID ANYMORE

Ms. T

Finding Myself

It is going to take a while
for me to find myself. But
I'm going to do it. Every day
I wake up, I will pray and ask
the Lord to give me strength
for my day, shine through me
and give me the fruit of the spirit
wisdom, knowledge. Open my ears
and eyes to know the difference.

Peace is what you get when you pray every daylight

What Happened to Me?

I BELIEVE I LOST MYSELF when I was twenty-two or twenty-three.
I started doing drugs, lost my children. Been through men who

beat on me. I lost my self-esteem, and it took a long time to get it back. Right now, today, I don't know what happened to me. I pray that it's gone and the pain will never come back. I carry a pain still over my children, that I don't have them in my life. I'm praying that I will get them back. That is the main thing I'm missing in my life.

Letter to Fear

I'm not afraid anymore.
Being afraid held me back for a long time.
Fear kept me from living,
doing the things I always wanted to do, fear.
Fear, I'm not afraid of you anymore, this time I claim joy.
Joy brings happiness to my heart.
You, fear, brought me pain, so much pain.
I have a new love now and it has brought me so much joy.
A roof over my head, a job, love all around me.
My family, my children and friends see the peace I have
and most of all my God shines through me.
I'm seeking Jesus again, this time nothing can stop me,
only Death. And I want to live forever.
I lost myself a long time ago and that's when fear took over
and it stayed with me for a long time.
I did not want to try anything new.
Didn't want to get my God or find a job.
I just gave up on everything and that is no way to live.
Fear is like stopping living, nowhere to go, nothing to do, just loss.
But since I have been here I made a big change in my life
and it feels so good. I'm starting to love myself
all over again. Since I let you go, fear.
I was afraid to get my children back.
But now I'm not. Fear can stop you
from having a lot of things, and doing a lot of things.

No more. I speak out now. I feel
and don't hold anything back and that feels good.
Thank you God for never giving up on me.
I'm getting my own place and that's a big step
for me. Never had my own place.
Not afraid, not no more.

LA HISTORIA DE MI VIDA

Yaritza Ortiz

Translated by Emily Polanco and Penny Saltsman

CUANDO APENAS TENÍA DOS MESES de nacida, sucedió que me dio una convulsión que ocasionó un daño al lado izquierdo del cerebro, afectando el lado derecho del cuerpo. Afectó mi desarrollo motor, entiéndase por la coordinación y el aprendizaje. Al afectarse el desarrollo motor, también se afectó el crecimiento; comencé a gatear y caminar tarde. Al gatear, arrastraba la pierna derecha; al caminar viraba la pierna, y mientras crecía, caminaba con la parte de afuera del pie. Entonces fue cuando comenzaron mis tratamientos con los médicos neurólogos, fisiatras y ortopedas, los cuales diagnosticaron mi condición como Hemiparesia Derecha (paralisia parcial del lado derecho).

A la edad de cinco años, comencé la escuela en kindergarten, donde mis padres comenzaron a luchar por mi futuro. En la escuela me comenzó a tratar un psicólogo, el cual siempre decía cosas negativas a mis padres. Las primeras noticias negativas que me dio fue un diagnóstico erróneo, diciendo a mis padres que yo tenía hiperactividad, y me dio un medicamento para tratar dicha condición. Mi madre comenzó a darme el medicamento, y cierto día la maestra se reunió con mi madre para hablar de lo que ocurría conmigo. La maestra la dijo a mi madre que me notaba retraída, callada y diferente a como era antes de comenzar los medicamentos, y fue cuando me quitaron el medicamento. Por segunda ocasión el psicólogo le volvió a dar otra noticia negativa, diciendo que lo mejor para mí era que me sacaran de la escuela porque yo nunca iba a pasar de grado (y hoy soy una persona preparada con un grado asociado y un grado técnico).

A la edad de trece años, me intervinieron quirúrgicamente en el pie derecho, haciendo un cruce de tendones para poder enderezar el pie. En lo largo de mi vida, me tuve que enfrentar al acoso por parte de mis compañeros de escuela, los cuales a diario se burlaban de mí por mi condición, y también me tuve que enfrentar a diferentes personas que no saben de la condición y que me decían cosas que me hacían sentir mal. Pero también hubo personas importantes que marcaron mi vida con su apoyo y su ayuda, a los cuales hoy les debo mi vida. Esas personas son mi familia, mis padres y hermanos; aparte de ellos hubo maestros de escuela y profesores de la universidad. Sin mi familia y mis profesores, no hubiera logrado graduarme de la universidad.

En la vida, uno comete errores que le marcan para siempre; a la edad de treinta años conocí un hombre, el cual estuve conociendo por dos años, y tome la mala decisión de irme de mi casa a vivir con él, creyendo que lo conocía. Él no me maltrató físicamente, pero sí verbalmente me humillaba, diciendo cosas feas de mí a los ocho meses. En el 2012 decidí terminar esa relación, y me vine con mis padres para los Estados Unidos, en los cuales estuve viviendo con ellos en la cuidad de Milwaukee, Wisconsin. Luego en el 2013 decidí mudarme para Indianápolis, Indiana, donde conocí al padre de mi hijo, al cual también, sin conocerlo suficiente, le di mi confianza, y fue cuando comenzó mi infierno a los tres meses de conocerlo. En marzo 2014 quedé embarazada, y creyendo en sus palabras de que se iba a ocupar de mí y de su hijo, me fui a vivir con él. A los cinco meses de embarazo él me comenzó a maltratar tanto físicamente como mentalmente, delante de su hijo de siete años. Pensé en varios ocasiones abandonarlo, pero en el maltrato emocional, empezó a amenazarme con amenazas que cada vez me daban temor, y decidía quedarme, pensando que todo iba a cambiar. El maltrato iba aumentando, pero dentro de todo ese sufrimiento llegó el día que me hizo muy feliz: el 22 de noviembre 2014 nació mi alegría, mi felicidad, mi hijo, y de ese día en adelante aunque seguían los maltratos, cada vez que yo miraba a mi bebé desde los tres meses de nacido, él me daba una sonrisa diciendo "Mamá, no te preocupes. Todo va a estar bien."

En agosto y septiembre 2015 sucedieron dos sucesos en los cuales decidí: no más maltrato. En septiembre 2015 decidí detener la violencia domestica cuando el 22 de septiembre a las medianoche de la madrugada me vi al borde de la muerte. Entonces fue cuando salí de la casa con mi hijo y comencé a vivir con mi familia de nuevo en Milwaukee. Luego en enero 2016, tuve que regresar a Indianápolis a vivir en un hogar para mujeres maltratadas donde pasaron buenos y malos momentos, pero también donde me enseñaron a combatir la violencia doméstica, y me ayudaron a superar muchos traumas. Hoy estoy volviendo a la normalidad de mi vida con mi hijo y mi familia porque gracias le doy a Dios que me trajo a mi hermano que vivía en Puerto Rico a vivir acá en Milwaukee y hoy puedo disfrutar de ver a mi hijo creciendo junto a toda mi familia. Aunque todavía el proceso judicial no ha terminado hoy, me siento libre y más que feliz, y sé que mi hijo también es feliz porque mi familia, sus abuelos, tíos y primos me ayudan con su crianza. Y sobre todo, sé que nos aman.

The Story of My Life

WHEN I WAS BARELY TWO months old, I suffered a seizure that caused damage to the left side of my brain, affecting the right side of my body. It impacted my motor development, and thus my coordination and my learning. As my motor development was affected, so was my growth: I began to crawl and walk late. When I crawled, I dragged my right leg; when I walked, I turned my leg, and as I grew, I walked with the outside of my foot. That was when I began treatment with neurologists, psychiatrists, and orthopedists, who diagnosed my condition as right hemiparesis (partial paralysis of the right side).

At the age of five, I started school in kindergarten, where my parents began fighting for my future. At school, I began treatment with a psychologist who always said negative things to my parents. The first bad news he gave me was a misdiagnosis, telling my parents that I had hyperactivity, and he gave me medication for that condition.

My mother started giving me the drug, and one day my teacher met with my mother to talk about what was happening with me. The teacher told my mother that she noticed I was withdrawn, quiet and different than I was before I started the drugs, and that's when they took me off the medicine. For the second time, the psychologist came back with more bad news, saying that the best thing for me was to take me out of school because I was never going to pass to the next grade (and now I am trained with an associate's degree and a technical degree).

When I was thirteen years old, they intervened surgically, crossing the tendons in my right foot so that I could straighten my foot. Through the course of my life, I had to face bullying from my classmates who mocked me daily for my condition, and I've also had to face different people who don't know about my condition and who have said things to me that made me feel bad. But there were also important people who left their mark on my life with their support and assistance, to whom I owe my life today. Those people are my family, my parents and siblings; apart from them, there were school teachers and college professors. Without my family and my teachers I would not have been able to achieve what I have and graduate from college.

In life, you make mistakes that mark you forever; when I was thirty, there was a man whom I had known for two years, and I made the bad decision to leave home to live with him, believing that I really knew him. He did not mistreat me physically, but he did humiliate me verbally, saying ugly things about me for those eight months. In 2012, I decided to end the relationship, and I came with my parents to the United States, where I was living with them in the city of Milwaukee, Wisconsin. Then in 2013, I decided to move to Indianapolis, Indiana where I met the father of my son, to whom (again, without knowing him well enough) I gave my trust, and that was when I began my hell, after three months of knowing him. In March 2014 I became pregnant and, believing his words that he would take care of me and his son, I went to live with him. When I was five months pregnant, he began to abuse me, physically as well as mentally, in front of his seven-year-old son.

I thought about leaving on several occasions, but with his emotional abuse he would make threats every time I wanted to leave that made me apprehensive, and I decided to stay, thinking that everything would change. The abuse was increasing, but in the middle of all that suffering came the day that made me very happy: on November 22, 2014, my joy, my happiness, my son was born, and from that day forward, although the mistreatment continued, every time I looked at my baby, from three months of age, he gave me a smile saying "Mama, don't worry. Everything is going to be fine."

In August and September of 2015, two events occurred, and I decided: no more abuse. In September 2015, I decided to end the domestic violence when, on September 22nd at midnight, I was on the verge of death. That was when I left home with my son and started living with my family again, back in Milwaukee. Then in January 2016, I had to return to Indianapolis to live in a home for battered women where there were both good and bad times, but where I was taught to combat domestic violence and they helped me overcome many traumas. Today I am returning to normality in my life with my son and my family. I give thanks to God, who brought my brother, who was living in Puerto Rico, to live here in Milwaukee, and today I enjoy seeing my son grow together with all my family. Although the legal process is not over yet, I feel free and more than happy, and I know my son is also happy because my family, grandparents, aunts and uncles and cousins help me with his upbringing. And above all, I know that they love us.

Si Yo Fuera un Águila

SI YO FUERA UN ÁGUILA yo fuera fuerte, libre, podría alcanzar metas inalcanzables. Sin miedo tomaría cada reto que se me enfrentara en la vida. Podría caminar libre sin sentir que me persiguen, sin sentir que necesito de alguien para que me guíe. Lograría mi libertad, podría ver más allá de la muralla que está frente a mí, y sobre todo sería completamente libre.

Yo quisiera poder ser yo sin tener a nadie que me diga que hacer quisiera tener la libertad de escoger a quien amar, a quien querer sin ser presionada o sin tener que dejar de amar para complacer a los demás. Sin embargo sé que tengo que dejarme guiar por aquel que me dio la vida, aquel que siendo como soy me ama sin medidos, aquel que no me pregunta porqué lo haces o porque no me escuchas, aquel quien no importando si le fallo me ama de igual manera y a quien hoy le debo mi vida, mi único amigo verdadero, el único que no se enoja conmigo y quien me protege a cada instante de mi vida, quien me da regalos sin yo merecerlo y quien cuida de mí en mi despertar y mi acostar; quien me cuida a mis amigos y familia a quien amo aunque en ocasiones le fallo y a quien siempre pido que no me deje, ni suelte mi mano, a ese ser que muchos ignoran, que muchos dicen que no existe y que muchos atropellan cada día con sus palabras, ese ser que un día dio su vida en una cruz y que día tras día nos ama y nos perdona sin pedir nada a cambio, ese ser se llama Jesús.

If I Were an Eagle

IF I WERE AN EAGLE, I would be strong, free; one that could reach unreachable goals. I would take every challenge that confronted me in life without fear. I would walk free, without feeling persecuted, without feeling that I need someone to guide me. I would achieve my freedom if I could see beyond the wall that is in front of me. Above all else, I would be completely free.

I would like to be without anyone telling me what to do; I would like to have the freedom to choose who to love and to love someone without being pressured or without having to stop loving someone to please others.

But I know that I have to let myself be guided by him who gave me life, someone that, even with me being the way that I am, loves me without measure; he who doesn't ask me why do you or don't you listen to me, someone that doesn't care if I fail. He loves me the same. And to whom, today, I owe my life, my only true friend, the only one that didn't get angry with me and who desired the best for me, who protected me every moment of my life, who gave me gifts I didn't deserve, and who took care of me in my waking and my sleeping; who cares for my friends and family, and who I love, although sometimes I fail him. And who I always ask not to leave me, nor let go of my hand, to that person that many have ignored, that many say doesn't exist, and that many run over every day with their words, the being who one day gave his life on a cross and who day after day, loves us and forgives us without asking for anything in return, that being is named Jesus.

Yo Recuerdo

YO RECUERDO EL DÍA QUE sentí que mi cuerpo había cambiado, ese día algo me decía que había un ser dentro de mí. Luego recuerdo el día que estaba en el hospital y el médico me dijo "felicidades, usted va a ser madre." Ese día mi vida se llenó de felicidad porque el sueño más anhelado se había cumplido.

Otra cosa que recuerdo fue el día en que nació mi bebe. Recuerdo ese día porque él estuvo en mis brazos pero no lo sentí ya que no había estado inconsciente, pero si me sedaron por el dolor y no tuve el privilegio en ese momento de sentir y acariciar a mí bebe. Pero también hubo alegría porque después y hasta el día de hoy, aun en medio de la tormenta que viví con el padre del niño, cada vez que lo miro el me da una sonrisa y es como si me dijera "mama todo va a estar bien".

El día que nació mi bebe tuve sentimientos encontrados ya que rompí fuente por la mañana y mi bebe nació en la tarde. En ese periodo de tiempo yo estaba más feliz porque ya iba a ser madre e iba a tener a mi bebe en mis brazos. Pero también fue doloroso ya que me fueron provocando los dolores. En medio de todo eso, jamás me imagine que mi bebe creciera sin su padre. Cuando el tiempo fue pasando estaba ansiosa, pues me daba mucho miedo por mi bebe. Cuando al fin nació, pensé que iba a disfrutar ese momento pero me medicaron y no pude sentir a mi bebe en ese momento. Pero a pesar de todo, ya mi bebe tiene uno año y desde sus tres meses me miraba con ternura y sonreía y para mi me está hablando diciéndome, "Mama, todo va a estar bien." Él ha sido el motor que ha mantenido mi vida corriendo, que me ha mantenido de pie, y cada día seguiré luchando por esa "Gotita de Felicidad" que Dios me regaló.

I Remember

I REMEMBER THE DAY I felt that my body was changing. That day, something told me that there was a being inside of me. Then I remember the day that I was in the hospital and the doctor told me, "Congratulations, you are going to be a mother." That day my life filled up with happiness because the fondest dream had come true.

Another thing that I remember is the day my baby was born. I remember that day because he was in my arms, but I couldn't feel him yet. I hadn't been unconscious, but they had sedated me for the pain, and I didn't have the privilege in that moment to hold and caress my baby. But there was also happiness because afterwards and up until today—even in the midst of the storm that I lived with his father—each time that I looked at him, he gave me a smile, as if he were saying to me, "Mama, everything is going to be okay."

The day that my baby was born, I had mixed feelings, already. My water broke in the morning, and my baby was born in the afternoon. In that period of time, I was the happiest, because I knew that I was going to be a mother, and I was going to have my baby in my arms. It was arduous, and caused me great physical pain. In the middle of it all, I never imagined my baby would grow up without his father. As the time passed, I was anxious and very afraid for my baby. When he was finally born, I thought I was going to enjoy that moment, but they medicated me, and I couldn't snuggle my baby right away.

My baby is now one-year old, and since he was three months old, he has looked at me tenderly and smiled at me in that way of his, as if saying, "Mama, everything is going to be okay." He is the motor that has kept my life going, and has kept me standing. Each day I will continue to fight for the "little drop of happiness" God has given me.

¿Quién Soy Yo?

YO SOY UNA PERSONA QUE quisiera ser más fuerte, más independiente, soy aquella persona que confía en las personas porque no sé cómo desconfiar. Quisiere a veces ser dura con las demás personas para no ser lastimada pero cuando intento hacerlo no sé cómo hacerlo. Soy una persona que me gusta ayudar a todo el mundo cuando sé que yo necesito ayuda, en ese momento yo no importe, importa la persona que necesita de mi ayuda, no sé cómo ser indiferente y siempre en mi mente pienso en las demás personas y me olvido que yo existo. Soy aquella persona que tiene metas pero metas en ayudar a las demás personas mi sueño y meta siempre ha sido ayudar a las personas desamparadas, maltratadas, y los niños, jóvenes y ancianos, me propone una meta y es en un futuro crear un centro donde halla amor, comprensión, donde seamos una familia, sin mirar raza, color, cultura, un hogar donde las puertas están abiertas a todos los necesitados. Sé que es difícil pero en este proceso he aprendido que por más difícil que sea el camino siempre debemos confiar en nosotros mismos, mirando siempre hacia adelante y cerrando tus oídos a todos los que quieran detenerte caminar sin detenernos, y no mirando lo que dejaste atrás, olvidando el pasado y manteniendo tu mente en el presente y el futuro y así veras cumplidos todos tus sueños y metas.

Yo sé que lo lograre, que este suceso en mi vida me enseno a tener confianza y fe en mí y con esta amarga experiencia, podre ayudar a otras personas en la misma situación. Ya estoy a mitad del camino, no ha sido fácil, lo que he recorrido. He sufrido y he llorado, me han lastimado y me han apoyado y gracias a eso estoy aquí más fuerte que nunca, tratando de ser la madre que mi hijo necesita. Sé que a veces no sé cómo hacerlo pero Dios siempre envía personas que me ayudan a dar ese paso que por miedo a no saber hacerlo no lo doy.

Who Am I?

I AM A PERSON THAT would like to be stronger, more independent; I am someone who always puts my trust in others because I don't know how to distrust. Sometimes I wish I could be stronger with other people in order to not get hurt, but when I try to do it I don't know how. I am someone who likes to help everyone, even when I know that I am the one who needs help at that moment. It doesn't matter—what matters is the person who needs my help. I don't know how to be indifferent, and I always put others first. I forget that I exist.

I am someone with goals, but the goals are to help other people. My dream has always been to help other people who are unfortunate and treated badly, to help children, youth, and the elderly. In the future, I want to create a center where there is love and understanding, where we can all be family without looking at race, color, culture; a home where the doors are open to everyone that needs it. I know that it would be difficult, but in this process I've learned that as difficult as it can all be, we should always trust in each other, always look forward, closing our ears to anyone that wants to stop us. Walk without stopping, and don't look at what you left behind. Forget the past and keep your mind on the present and the future. That's how you will see all of your wishes and goals come true.

I know that I will achieve my goals. This bitter experience in my life has shown me to trust and have faith in myself. I can help other people in the same situation. I am now in the middle of the path. What I've travelled hasn't been easy; I've suffered, and I've cried. Some have hurt me, and some have supported me. And thanks to it all, I am here, stronger than ever, trying to be the mother my son needs. I know that sometimes I don't know how to do it, but God always sends people to help me, to step away from the fear that I don't know what to do.

My happiest memory is of when my baby was born; within that happy story, there was a strong moment for me. When my baby was born, I was drugged, and while it was in my system I couldn't feel very well or hold my baby. It's hard for me to speak about it because that's the most anticipated moment for a mother. Being unable to hug or tend to my baby made me powerless. I cried the day my husband finally put my baby in my arms because for me it was as if my baby was just born. I relished it. I took care of him and didn't let go of him for many hours.

When my baby was discharged, I arrived home to a brand new experience. He was my first baby, and to hear him cry was so distressing. They told me, "Leave him alone. He has to learn and grow." When my baby was six months old he began to sit up. I was afraid that he would get hurt or that something would happen to him, and my husband always said that he had to grow up. It was difficult for me to conceive of letting him go, to grow up. He was my baby; how was I to understand that a person so little was going to learn so quickly.

• *Art by Stevie Richardson* •

LOST IN LOVE

Whys

I REMEMBER WHEN I WAS young how there were so many things we went through in life like having water, gas, phone, or lights being cut off at different times, and I never really understood why it was, but we made the best of it. I also remember when the water man came to cut off our water my mom would fill our washing machine with water so we could wash up for school.

My mom had three kids, including me. I started to be an angry child and began hanging around with the wrong people so I could learn ways to make money to help my mom, sister, and brother out so we could have things. I stayed angry with my mom for us being poor. I was only fifteen.

By the time I turned thirty-five, I learned that she had a bad accident when she was seventeen: her stepsister chased her out of the house and she was hit by some sort of vehicle, but my grand-mother never got the treatment my mother needed, and she was somewhat delayed mentally. That made my hard heart feel bro-ken—to never know that until I was this old. Nonetheless, I un-derstood everything much better, and I get that because of her mother, my grandmother, she never got the treatment she needed.

I see that she tried very hard to raise us three kids. I tried to be better as a daughter to her, when I was older, by helping her out more, but still to this day she is an angry woman. She treats my sister and brother much better than she treats me. It's like she doesn't like me. My younger sister is her favorite child, and that's okay. I have learned to let that go. I even let my sister and brother go, because they bring me down so much, and try not to have a relationship, due to the things I have done in the past, which were things to help them out. All I did as a teenager and young adult was to do wrong things for myself and my family. We were very poor growing up. I had a child at the early age of eighteen, and I took care of her the best way that I could: by breaking the chain my grandmother and mother had in their relationship. Me and my daughter have a bond that is beyond the universe, we are so close, that I am just now teaching myself that I have to let her go. I just get scared that I haven't taught her enough in this horrible world, but she says that I taught her too much to be a nineteen year-old, so I will let her go and experience life for herself, without me. It's really difficult to do when you love your child so much. I really do believe she will be okay.

It's just me and her for now. All of my immediate family left me or disowned me due to the choices I have made. I prayed a lot and forgave them, but forgiveness hasn't been both ways, yet. So, yes, I have let my family go. That led me to a "friends-with-benefits" dysfunctional type of deal with a man that got bad pretty quickly, and sent me on a journey unlike anything I have been through before in my life.

I was beyond scared to go this way with my child. However, the Julian Center is a blessing God sent. At this place, I've met people who helped me more than my family. I was terrified at first, but as the months go on, it's become home, help, love, and a place that has so many resources for me to use for free.

I have been at the Julian Center for three months, almost, and I'm slowly growing. That's the best feeling ever: to know you are changing for the better. My daughter is also changing since being at the center. Having an advocate has taught me to be more accountable for my responsibilities, like when I drop the ball and miss appointments or classes. I really appreciate that, because in the past I never made mistakes like that. I was always on top of everything. Being at the center is helping me reclaim who I used to be before having negative personal relationships, and negative family relationships. I so badly want to return to the person I was before all of this.

My Family Tree

I was mistaken when I thought a tree and its branches was another way of thinking about family. Or even meaning another way to describe how families connect. I always thought it started with the roots, then the stump, next the body, and lastly the branches. However, that is one of the biggest myths I've heard yet!

I don't know about your family, but my family is a half dead tree with no roots, no branches connecting, and no matter what the season is, you'll never see a leaf on it.

I love trees and when I see one I just stand in front of it staring smiling, and touching it, along with taking in the fresh air. As soon as I think of family I see a sick, poisoned, rotted bark that would fall if a baby kicked it.

Family = (fools) (assholes) (monsters) (illiterate) (living half-dead) yucko.

I know that sounds mean and harsh, however, it's more loving than you think. What you put out is what you get back. Although I love them they are a dead tree that I will be cutting down as soon as I get the money to buy a saw.

A chainsaw, that is.

Confessions

I.

I remember the day I got baptized and confessed my sins. It was mind-blowing. Even more so as I think back on how I was able to share that moment with my daughter, not to mention my first cousin, along with her husband and children.

I got very serious with worship and started to learn more and more. For weeks all I could think about was being so scared to walk down into the water.

Now I only think of how my Pastor at that time dipped me into the water and brought me back up. It was beyond the world.

II.

I wish my cousin was never murdered. I wish I hadn't seen so much domestic violence in my life, in my family's life, resulting in their deaths. I wish I didn't have to experience the death of friends. I wish the last call he made was not to me. I wish during those times, during the 80s, I had the knowledge to recognize a person who plans to kill themselves. I wish I could stop wishing that someone makes a time machine so I could go back and save family and friends. I wish I didn't see his body dead on the floor.

III.

I'm having a moment where I feel like a helpless bird in a cage, just sitting there watching everyone else walk by me and say the strangest things to me—so they can get a laugh out of it. Like the whole plan was to make a fool out of me or make sure that I could never fly out of here on my own unless she gave me the key.

How Did I Get Here?

How did I get here to this point where I'm living at the shelter, and having no one in my life except those who work with me on my case at the shelter, the few friends I have made here and, most importantly, God and my daughter.

I've decided to take a step back with my thinking. I'm always thinking, and since I can't stop thinking, ever, maybe I would have success turning back my thoughts to try and think where things went wrong with me. As I think back, I think of the happiest times in my life about twenty years ago, when I gave birth to my only child. That's when I felt real love. That was when I wanted a better life: to go back and finish school and then go to college. I wanted to be a better parent and for my child to have both of her parents since I didn't. I wanted to be an all-around better person.

I became what I wanted. At some point I lost it all by making bad choices and putting myself in a mind-frame that when I did bad things, I had no other choice. Maybe that wasn't true, but it felt true at the time.

As I think back, I know it was wrong, but I still can't say that I had other options. One thing that has never changed is that I have never felt like anybody loved me. I was the firstborn for both my parents, but they both started having other children, and I was the one who received less love and less support and was always pushed to the side. I used to tell myself that my parents had a hard time showing their emotions, but that isn't true because I watched them love my sisters and brothers unconditionally. They both loved them no matter what.

My mother had three children, two girls and a boy. My sister and brother are still her everything, and the love she gives me is nowhere near half of what she gives them. I always thought it was because I was a troubled teen, always giving them problems and having personal problems and going to juvenile detention center three or four times. I used to do things to make up for being a bad child. I guess in my head I thought making up or trying to make up would earn me the same love as my sister and brother, but it didn't.

Currently the only difference is my mother and her other children love me even less. My sister, who is my mother's youngest, loves me half of the time and dislikes me the other half. And my brother simply hates me all the time and for the most part never cared about me. In my mind I was okay with it for two reasons: they were all I had, and now I have this child that loves me, so it was okay that my immediate family didn't love me.

My mom has a small family, one sister and one brother. Her sister loved me as a kid and hated me as an adult. I honestly don't know why, but I have been learning to pray and keep going. I haven't seen my uncle since I was seven or eight. I don't know if he just disappeared or what, but he was always nice to me. My mother had several half-sisters that always showed they liked me and never treated me bad. They were always kind to me but I was never able to get close to them because my mom never went around them. I always wondered why but didn't understand until I was close to forty. I was thirty-seven. Throughout my mom's family I had a cousin or two that cared for me, and that was about it.

My dad likes me, I know it to be true, but he didn't love me like his other children. That's how I have always felt, back then and currently. My siblings on my dad's side liked me but didn't love me like they loved each other. I do think that it's because I have a different mom than the rest, so they love their whole siblings the best, and I am just a half. I understand why they love me less and am okay with it, but I want them to treat me the same as a whole sibling.

But, again, maybe it was because of me having a roller coaster life. Things were always going for me, but when I made stops, I made them at different places: bad-kids stop, bad-teenager stop, getting-into-trouble stop, getting-my-life-on-track stop, becoming-a-better-person stop, getting-and-learning-I-was-depressed stop, anxiety stop, becoming-distant stop, back to depression stop, make-bad-choices-with-me stop, back to the depression stop, then back to getting-in-trouble stop, depression-and-anxiety-again stop, then the homeless stop, not to mention all the stops I can't remember.

I guess all those stops I made made my family love me less

and less. I guess they just got tired of me having so many issues in my life. Hell, I'm tired, past tired. I'm just here, literally trying to figure life out. The only difference is I have to do it alone, and that's okay, because I have to do it no matter what happens, and no matter who cares for me, no matter when I get to the right stop. I just have to get there for my child and myself. What no one seems to get is I only want to get to the correct path, to the right stop for me and my daughter. As I learn more about myself, and the things I have done to get me here, at this bad place in my life, it's because of the choices I made. I'm not saying I got here because I was unloved. That's not how I feel, I'm just trying to revisit my feelings and thoughts. I made all my bad decisions and choices on my own. I guess I feel like, by writing this, it will help me gain some understanding of who I was and who I have become. Having hope that I can make it back, not to who I was as "great," but make a new me, a better me, than who I was.

Why

Why do we dream of each other
Why do we scream at each other
Why don't we talk to each other
Why don't I love myself properly
Why do I have a hard time saying bye
Why do I accept bad things
Why don't I love me more
Why do I attract bad people
Why does that make me think I'm bad
Why do bad things happen
Why can't I stop my heart from aches
Why do I want to cry
Why do I dream of this
Letting go is hard for me
Why?

Lie

I lie a lot, I want to stop
When I lie I feel safe
Lies protect me from others
Lies make me happy
Lies let me stay hidden
My lies are my truth
I believe my lies
My lies are love…to me
Why are my lies a safe place for me
I use lies to walk away
I love my lies
I hate that I love my lies
Why don't I stop the lies
I let others lie to me
I laugh when I hear lies
I cry because I lie
Lies are all I do
I love to lie
I lie a lot, I want to stop
I don't want to lie but I feel I have to.

A Letter to My Mother

DEAR….
I'm so confused on how to address this fucking letter. Even though we are on good terms now, or maybe just a place where we are playing nice and bullshitting one another. Still, it leaves me double-blinking—what to say. With that being said, I will say:

Dear my friend,

Since you were my friend first, and I will always respect you, no matter what you've done, or will do, to me. I guess that comes from me being cut from a different tree.

The thing that gets to me is how you always put me last. I was never first with you for anything, unless I had several $20 bills to give you. Then you would try to be best friends with me....

I didn't like how she was basically trying to be best friends with my friends. My friends would come over to my house at times, and ask her sex questions, or just to talk about sex, or to tell her when they had sex. Yet she never taught me about sex. If she had, I probably never would have made so many bad choices.

Don't misunderstand me—one of my bad choices gave me a real reason to live, and be a better me. And that's what I have done.

Once I got my life together and earned a degree on my own, got the job and the place I wanted—when all that happened, my mom began to call me and ask for money and favors. I gave her whatever she wanted. I learned that what I gave was never enough for her. As soon as I stopped being generous, things went south, and she went right back to acting like we were just friends.

My sister was pretty much the same, except she was so busy, worried about her weight, she didn't have much time to treat me bad, just on the weekends. Whenever I had an argument with my sister, my mom would always jump in and side with her. Every time. Without even knowing what happened. My fat sister is my crazy-ass mom's favorite person.

Prompt #1: I remember…

Prompt #2: I don't remember…

Prompt #3: I am [animal]…

Prompt #4: Before/After

Prompt #5: Write about a favorite place from the past…

Prompt #6: Write about someplace hidden…

Prompt #7: I was born…

Prompt #8: I am from…

Prompt #9: Tell the story of What I have kept / What I have lost / What I have found

Prompt #10: What I know / What I don't know / I wish I knew

Prompt #11: I release / I take / I give

Prompt #12: I am not afraid of / I am afraid of

Prompt #13: What you wanted… / What I wanted…

Prompt #14: You were mistaken when you… / I was mistaken when I…

Prompt #15: What do you wish never happened to you or someone you love?

Prompt #16: What about your own life do you feel that you will never understand?

Prompt #17: What enrages you?

Prompt #18: Was there some ideal time in your life to which you long to return?

Prompt #19: Pick a scar—one that is seen or unseen. Tell the story of that scar. What happened in the beginning, middle, end?

Prompt #20: Write about a time you healed—what was the process, describe the steps you had to take, and what you had to do. Is the healing complete? Tell the story.

Prompt #21: Write a picture of kindness in your life.

Prompt #22: Write a picture of a desolate time in your life.

Prompt #23: Tell the story of the first time someone hurt you, as you remember it. It can be physical or emotional.

Prompt #24: Tell the story of a day you were happy.

Prompt #25: Tell the story of how you came to be at the Julian Center.

Prompt #26: Tell the story of what life was like right before you came to the Julian Center. What is life like after coming to the Julian Center?

Prompt #27: What if...?

Prompt #28: A day in my life...

Prompt #29: Dear... (write a letter to someone or something of your life, or to yourself)

Prompt #30: Inside of me / Outside of me

Editor
Rachel Sahaidachny holds an M.F.A. in Creative Writing from Butler University. She is a poet and works as Programs Manager for the Indiana Writers Center. She was a workshop leader for the Butler University Writing for Wellness program, and also teaches for the Indiana Writers Center. Her series of six linked poems exploring a traumatic mother-child relationship was a finalist for the Coniston Prize from *Radar Poetry* (Issue 12). She is co-editor of *Not Like the Rest of Us: An Anthology of Contemporary Indiana Writers* and previously served as poetry editor for *Booth: A Journal*. Recent writing appears in *Southeast Review, Radar, Red Paint Hill, Nuvo,* and others.

Translations
Penny Saltsman is a graduate of Ball State University in Muncie, Indiana, where she studied Spanish Linguistics and Culture with a minor in German. As an undergraduate student, she earned a writing award for her primary research on obedience and conformity. Her series of essays on "the 'F' word," examining the modern relevance of the word "feminism," was selected for publication as sample writing for the university's Writing Proficiency Exam. Penny is a language enthusiast, a humanist, and an amateur-but fervent-ukuleleist. She currently resides in Indianapolis and works as an IT professional for Indiana University.

Book Designer
Andrea Boucher is currently earning her M.F.A. in Creative Writing from Butler University. In addition to writing creative nonfiction and teaching classes at the Indiana Writers Center, she also freelances as a book designer. She has done numerous covers and book designs for IWC.

Special thanks to the volunteers who came to support the workshop members, showing up every week to listen, write, transcribe, and build a stronger story: Amy Maria Demien, Andrea Boucher, BSU intern Billie MacTighe, Emily Polanco, Laura Kendall, Lorna Rose Simulis, Mary Redman, Thierry Menchhofer, and Tracy Line. Special thanks to Emily Polanco and Penny Saltsman for their work translating the stories from Spanish.

Special thanks to the Julian Center, Catherine O'Connor, Nathan Ferreira, Gina Baird, Christine Arthur, and Amanda Henemyre for helping coordinate and support the writing sessions.

And to the workshop participants: thank you for coming to write, for being courageous, mindful, and true, and trying something new. This book wouldn't be possible without you.